DARK BLUE BLOOD

SCOTTISH RUGBY
IN THE BLACK AND WHITE ERA

By Steve Finan

Heartfelt thanks to . . .

PUTTING a book together is never a quick or simple thing. A former editor (when I lived in the newspaper world) used to say that if you didn't have enough expertise to write authoritatively on a subject then find someone who does — doublequick. So I did.

Foremost among the people I must thank is Ian "Barney" Barnes, former Hawick lock and coach, and the owner of seven Scotland caps. He is pictured on page 219. When there were faces I did not recognise, I called upon Barney's encyclopaedic rugby brain. In times of even greater or more obscure need, Barney enlisted his son David Barnes (who runs the quite excellent offsideline. com website), or picked the brains of Hamish More, Hugh Pollock, Mack Brown, Gary Callander, Terence Froud, and Gareth "Hovis" Brown.

This book wouldn't have been much at all without their collective knowledge.

Kevin Janiak of The Southern Reporter supplied me with quite a few superb photos. And free coffee. I am also greatly in his debt.

Paul Brough, archive manager at Hawick Hub, and his team, also supplied excellent photos, as well as good advice and professional expertise.

Thanks are also due to:
    Stewart Weir.
    Leon Strachan.
    James Kirk.
    Craig Houston.
    Gill Martin.
    Sylwia Jackowska.
    Jacqui Hunter.
    David Powell.
    Barry Sullivan.
    Irina Florian.
    Kirsty Smith.
    Gary Thomas.
    Duncan Laird.
    Raymond Barr.
    Nikki Fleming.
    Deirdre Vincent.
    Carole Finan.
    Rebecca Finan.
    Lewis Finan.
    Fraser T. Ogilvie.

Last, but by no means least, great thanks must also go to the incomparable Doddie Weir for a superb foreword and a lot of happy rugby memories.

To buy any of the photos in this book, see page 300.

DARK BLUE BLOOD
SCOTTISH RUGBY
IN THE BLACK AND WHITE ERA

ISBN 978-1-84535-819-8

First published in Great Britain in 2020 by DC Thomson & Co., Ltd.,
Meadowside, Dundee, DD1 9QJ
Copyright © DC Thomson & Co., Limited.

Visit **www.dcthomsonshop.co.uk**
To purchase this book.
Or Freephone 0800 318 846 / Overseas customers call +44 1382 575580
Typeset & internal design by Steve Finan.
Cover design by Leon Strachan.

Foreword — the power

BEING asked to write the foreword for such a fantastic book, illustrating Scottish rugby through the years, may seem a strange choice given my history around photography – or more accurately photographers – when throughout my entire rugby career, and even in to retirement, I have heard the command: "And can you just come down a wee bit at the back, big yin?"

Naturally, I have always made it easy for the "snapper", but covering rugby – or any action sport for these guys – especially in times past, could never have been described as being easy.

While colour makes recognition simpler when it comes to identifying teams, matches and venues, there is something special about capturing the moment in black and white, or should that be grey, given some of our national team performances over the decades, or, just the weather, often dreich, muddy and miserable. But that's Scotland for you in winter – and spring, and autumn, even summer.

The invention of colour photography, and more recently, digital technology, has meant that few images today are shot purely in black and white. There was a time though, when that was the norm. You only have to visit one of the many clubhouses, committee rooms or bars (didn't take me long to arrive there, did it?) belonging to the various teams up and down the country to see the monochrome photographs in all their glory.

Players and officials wanted to have their biggest and best moments captured so that future generations might enjoy the imagery of past glories. Amongst those photos you will find the history of clubs, from their first origins on a field with posts at either end, to the building of grandstands and club facilities, which in their day were state of the art, but today, look like listed buildings.

Trophies and cups inevitably feature, as do those of players who achieved the ultimate accolade, to represent their country, from the one-cap wonders to the legends of Scottish rugby.

At the Greenyards, one wall is dedicated to those who wore the thistled jersey, resplendent with their first cap. It was, as I was reminded often enough coming through the ranks at Melrose, "Where you want to be."

Of course, there are other elements to these photographs, which although not obvious at the time, have certainly merited comment since. Like, what was that moustache thing all about? And who told you it suited you?

Or, when did that hairline become less about the hair? And, for most, that the lean, mean fighting machine isn't so lean and mean thirty or forty years on. And yet again, the vast majority captured in black and white.

I may have gone on to play for Scotland, and the Lions, and for Newcastle Falcons and Border Reivers. However, while it's fantastic

# of old photos

to take the acclaim, you never forget the time when you were just emerging at club level, making the breakthrough and being spoken about, and inevitably, the first real recognition you got was through your local newspaper.

A few words of praise made you feel ten feet tall (although, clearly, I was much taller than that), but a photograph, wow, now you had really made it.

My late mother collected every scrap, cutting or article from the publications printed around the Borders, singling out her favourites, often with a critical eye. Maybe, there was a frustrated picture editor in there desperate to get out. Her main complaint was that too often, even in joyous moments like scoring a try, I looked very serious. I don't think she fully appreciated that when you were being lifted miles in the air, smiling for the cameras wasn't your number one priority.

You might see that look of fear flicking through these pages.

There were some pictures though that she didn't just want in newsprint; she wanted the actual glossy photograph.

As a player, and today, I've always been happy to help the photographer, because ultimately, it gives you a bargaining chip when it comes to asking for one of their images. It might not be hung above the fireplace, and may go no further than the fridge, but it is a memory worth keeping.

Ultimately, that is what this book is about, the memories.

Lovers of rugby, be it players or punters, will see folk in this book they remember, and recall the names, places and friends that has made rugby such a fantastic game.

I hope you enjoy it.

Doddie Weir, 2020.

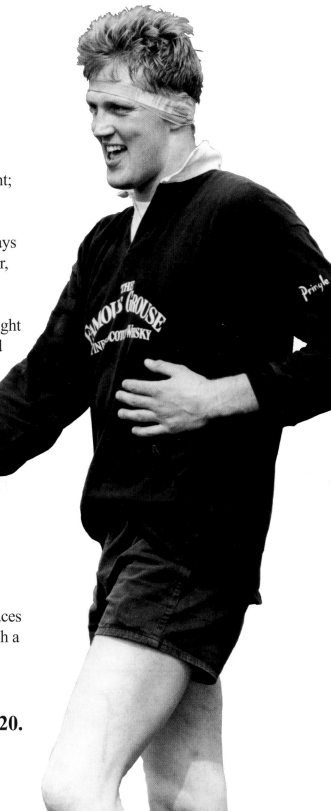

"B" Select Rugby Team

Gems from the archives

MOST of these photos have been hidden away in newspaper and magazine archives for decades. They have had long, and sometimes hard, working lives.

There may be crop marks where sports editors wanted cuts made, or had demanded head-and-shoulder shots of individual players. Some photos have had their background removed. Some have been clumsily re-touched. They were in use in the pre-digital age, when photo manipulation was done with chinagraph pencils and sprayguns.

It would have been nice to commission a photographer to get new shots, but he'd have to also be furnished with a time machine. The expense account didn't run to such extravagances.

So some of these shots are a little tattered round the edges. The lighting in others is a bit strange. Some don't quite have complete left-to-right captions. I make no apology for any

of that. These heirloom photos bear the scars of their existence in the long history of newspaper and magazine production.

The content of the photos, however, is young men in their prime and in their natural element. Their vitality and youth was captured and frozen for ever.

The men themselves, of course, aged, greyed and in many cases died long ago. But these photos show the way they were when they were full of vigour and eager to play the game they loved.

Neither is this a complete record of every team's achievements, nor does it show every great player who ever graced the game.

It would have been easy to fill a book with photos of internationals, or Scotland's Grand Slam victories. But that's been done before.

There is a substantial chapter on Scotland, but I have purposefully avoided making it a book only about

internationals. This is a book about nostalgia for the game. The way it was at all levels.

Some of the teams and players weren't ever champions. Some weren't even very good. But rugby is for everyone, not just the most skilled.

I purposefully and proudly display photos that will not be in any other book or collection.

I dug and delved among the back shelves of archives to find obscure and long-forgotten matches and faces.

If a book that celebrates the black and white era of rugby can do anything at all, it can showcase a few players who didn't stand out, didn't shine, but contributed a great deal to the sport.

The game belongs to them as much as anyone.

Steve Finan.

■ Hawick legend Wullie Gray.

CONTENTS

■ Scotland v.
South Africa 1961.

DARK BLUE BLOOD
SCOTTISH RUGBY
IN THE BLACK AND WHITE ERA

Chapter 1

The Old Grounds

THERE is no better way to start a book about rugby in the past than a look at the places where it was played. There are some special rugby places in Scotland. Our towns and cities have their own churches, from Mansfield Park to Seafield, and from Goldenacre to Netherfield.

There is something of a tribal warfare feel about going to another club's ground and taking a win.

But this will rarely be a simple matter. No team walks away from the likes of Jed-Forest's Riverside Park and says, "Well that was easy".

Rugby grounds are a reflection of their town and their people. Each has a character and a history. Pride in the team is part of the fabric.

All this adds to the occasion. A rugby town and a rugby ground on the day of a big game is a fine place to be.

■ **A packed Milntown for The Langholm Sevens.**

■ Gala's New Netherfield ground, was constructed in 1961-62, at a cost of £20,000. It was the first new rugby ground in Scotland for several decades.

■ Glasgow University v. Edinburgh University at the striking venue of the old Westerlands Playing Fields (before they were sold for housing). You don't see so many players wearing glasses during a game these days.

■ Edinburgh Academical v. London Scottish at Raeburn Place, the world's oldest rugby venue.

■ Two photos of Hawick's Mansfield Park taken from almost identical angles but a few years apart. One from the first half of the 1950s showing the old grandstand, the other with the new.

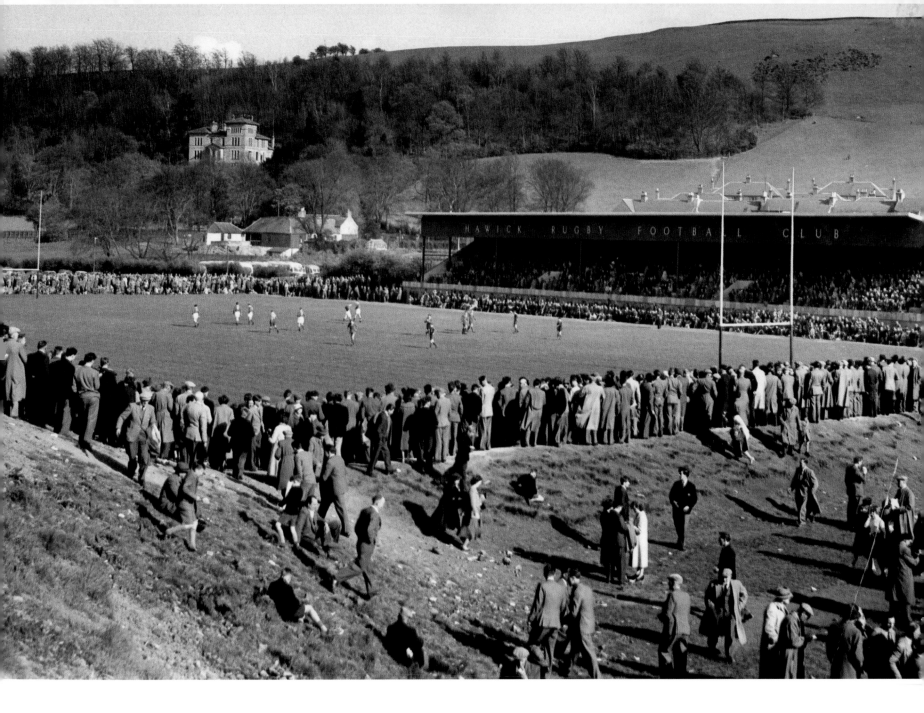

■ **The new stand, officially opened by SRU vice-president R.J. Hogg on New Year's Day 1957, before the traditional Ne-erday game v. Heriots (which Hawick won). It remains the biggest stand in the Borders area, seating 1,400 spectators.**

■ A closer view of the magnificent new stand at Mansfield Park in 1957.

■ The North Bank at Mansfield Park, which catches any sunshine that is available, has always been a great place from which to watch the Sports.

■ Heriot's FP First XV pictured at Goldenacre, season 1962-63. The ground is one of Scotland's most venerable and was overlooked in the sixties (as it still is) by the expensive real estate on Bangholm Terrace.

The 3,000-capacity Goldenacre Sports Ground is owned by George Heriot's School, which counts "greats" such as Ken Scotland, Andy Irvine, Iain and Kenny Milne and Bruce Douglas among its alumni.

Heriot's FP Rugby Club was formed in 1890, originally playing only former pupils, as many of the FP sides did.

This '62-63 FP team is, back, from left: Peter Wight, George Paterson, Derek McCracken, David Milne, Jimmy Simpson, Gil Borthwick, Norman Rushbrook, Peter Binnie.

Front: Bill Gardiner, George Shand, Colin Blaikie, John Ross (captain), Ian Palmer, Dave Binnie, Hamish More.

The last named, Hamish More, is one of many men, over the years, who played first-class cricket as well as being an accomplished rugby player.

He still holds the Scottish record for seven catches against the touring Pakistan side of 1971.

Rugby was often the sport that cricketers would play to keep their fitness up over the winter months.

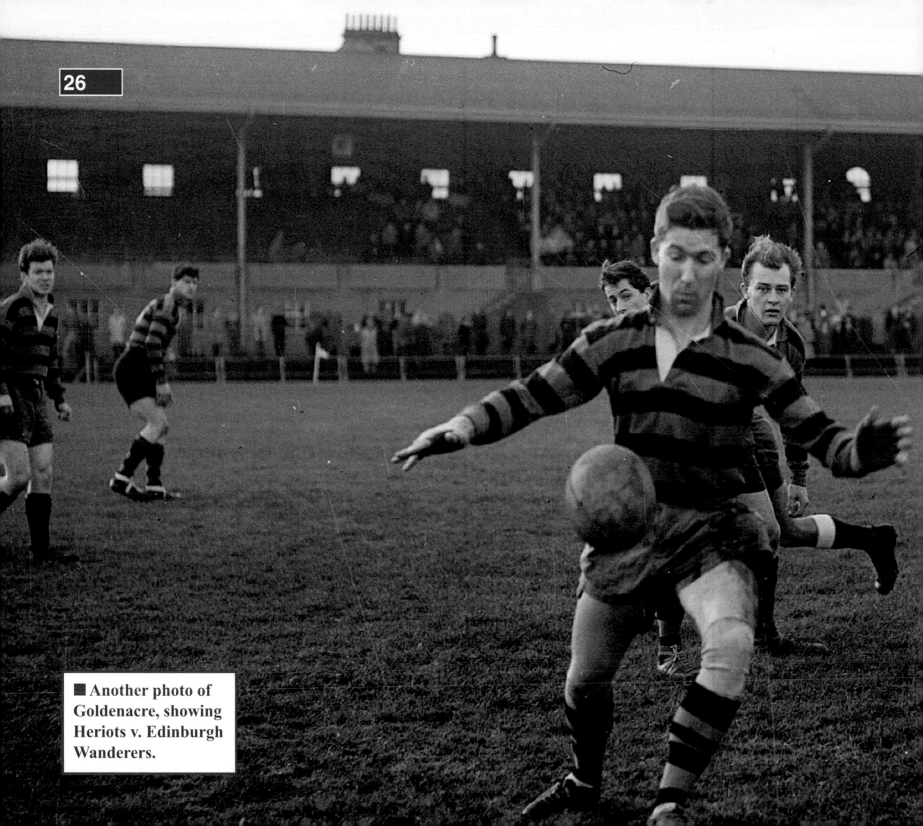

■ Another photo of Goldenacre, showing Heriots v. Edinburgh Wanderers.

■ Goldenacre again,
Heriots v. Gala, 1968.

■ Dundee University College visit Melrose on March 19th, 1952.

■ The All Blacks at Linksfield
Stadium Aberdeen, December
5th, 1978. NZ won 31-3.

■ **Derek Arnold scores a try for The All Blacks v. Edinburgh & Glasgow at Hughenden on November 20th, 1963. The New Zealanders won this one 33-3.**

■ A bird's eye view of the action at Gordon's College ground at Seafield, Aberdeen, on October 4th, 1980, during Gordonians RFC's first match in Division 1 of the Scottish Rugby Union Championship. The 1,500 crowd lining the pitch obviously lifted the home team, who beat Hawick 26-13.

■ **Melrose RFC's Greenyards, overlooked by the Eildons.**

■ New Myreside. Watsonians entertain Heriots in the early 1960s. From far left: John Ross (Heriots), Dizzie Kidd (Watsonians), Alan McNish (Watsonians), Graeme Orr (Watsonians), Derek McCracken (Heriots). Partially obscured behind John Stent (who has the ball) is Jimmy Simpson (Heriots) and far right the Herioter is Peter Binnie.

It is an indication of rugby's long history in general, and Watsonians' history in particular, that the "new" part of the ground's name is in reference to the club moving from their original Myreside, on what was then the outskirts of Edinburgh, not far to their current home . . . in 1933.

38

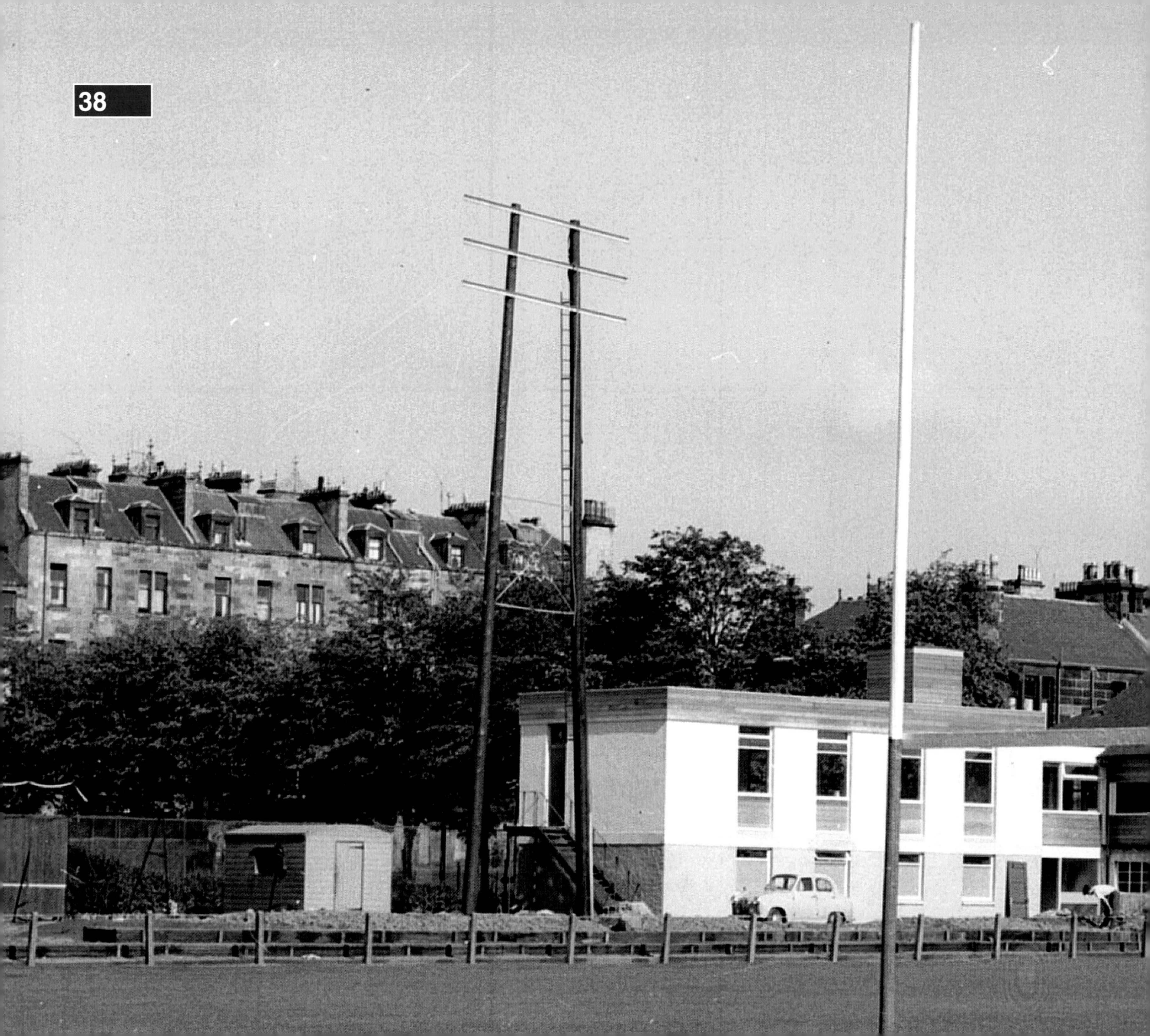

■ Floodlighting being installed in the 1960s alongside the pavilion at Hughenden, home of Hillhead RFC.

DARK BLUE BLOOD
SCOTTISH RUGBY
IN THE BLACK AND WHITE ERA

Chapter 2

Murrayfield. Home.

IT is the nation's home. Our stadium. It has history seeping out of the girders.

It opened in 1925, just in time for The Immortals (see page 148) to grace it. And from those early days, when there was one stand and three embankments, it has seen great endeavours and, it must be said, some crushing disappointments.

It is a Scottish landmark, the place where Scotland has tested itself against all the great teams.

It became an all-seater venue in 1993, but those with longer memories will recall the swaying, shouting, singing days when 104,000 squeezed in to the Scotland-Wales Five Nations encounter of 1971. That crowd is still a European record.

And it is a fine day out nowadays. The fan village is great fun, the stadium looks and feels wonderful, and the noise during a big game is deafening.

May the old lady live long and prosper.

■ **Murrayfield in 1991.**

■ The Scottish Football Union (as it was then called) was the first of the Home Unions to own a purpose-built rugby ground. That was at Inverleith in Edinburgh, less than a mile to the north-east of Murrayfield. The old stadium hosted matches from 1901.

But success demanded expansion and the original 19 acres where Murrayfield now stands was purchased from Edinburgh Polo Club in 1922. A debentures scheme raised enough money to build an impressive stadium.

The ground was officially opened as Scotland's new rugby venue on, March 21st 1925.

Due to demand for tickets in the years between the wars, two wing extensions to the central stand were added in 1936, giving the edifice its familiar three-part look that would remain until modern ground reconstruction nearly 60 years later. These wings increased the capacity to more than 15,000.

The debentures allocated seats to the same people for years at a time, and very quickly internationals at Murrayfield became social occasions. Though players on the pitch might change, off the field familiar faces became old friends who would meet season after season.

That old wooden stand was far from luxurious, and the seats were rather close together, but the place had character and many a good time and many a laugh was had in the old Murrayfield main stand, no matter what was happening on the pitch.

Though it was, at times, a wee bit cold . . .

■ Murrayfield's old main stand, and groundsman, and dog, in 1962.

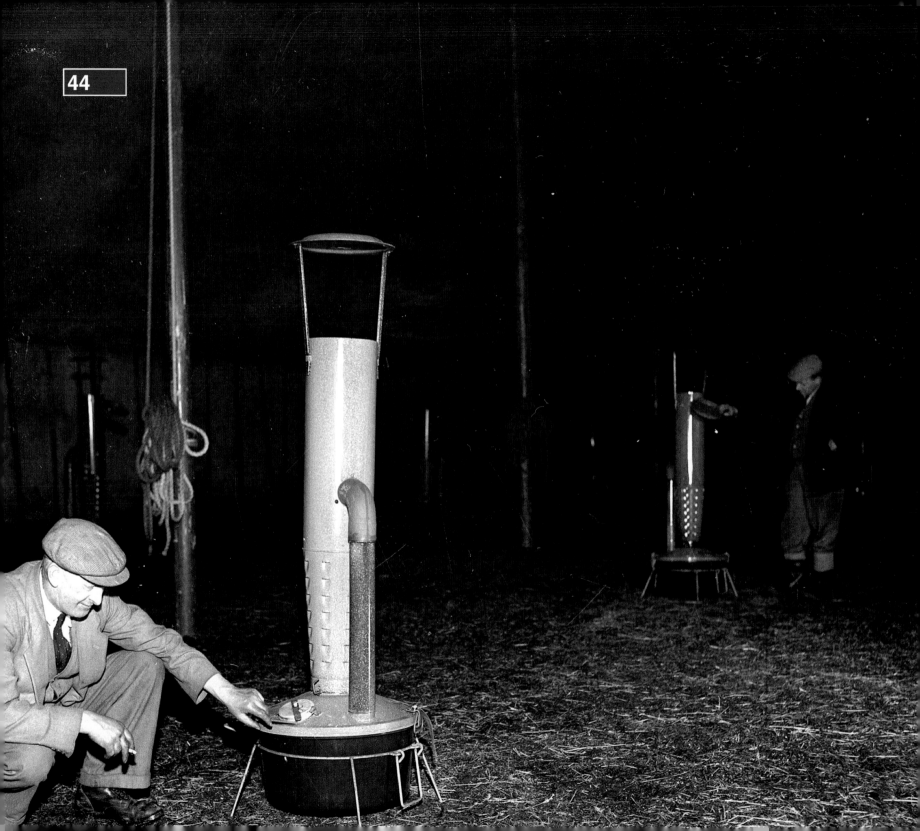

■ Getting the pitch playable was always a concern. The old system of paraffin heaters inside tents (left) was inadequate by the 1950s — and because it was coupled with spreading straw on the pitch, was a fire hazard. Whisky magnate Dr Charles Hepburn donated £10,000 in 1959 to purchase what was then called an electric blanket. Nowadays it would be termed undersoil heating. This was installed in 1960. But the network of pipes left the non-playing areas to the mercy of the elements, so this would be brushed away before games, as the above 1981 photo shows.

■ Anyone who ever sat through a game would advise a blanket and hot water bottle were essential equipment in the main stand.

This 1960s groundsman hardly needs to get down on hands and knees and plant a thermometer in the tundra to tell that the day might prove to be a trifle chilly.

■ The problem is that the rugby calendar has always scheduled Five Nations matches in Scotland's coldest months.

Big men, travelling at speed, thrown to the ground by robust tackles, requires a surface that isn't going to dislocate shoulders or fracture knee caps.

Keeping the surface soft enough to squash an Englishman into it often required hard work, enough straw to start a farm . . . and the cooperation of the weather gods.

■ Murrayfield's straw covering in February 1958.

50 ■ It was always a great place to watch rugby, though the terraces were a little shallow. Heaven help you if your view was obscured by a line of forwards up from the Borders for the day!

■ High jinks during the
1984 slam-winning match
with France.

■ The pitch is invaded during celebrations of the hoodoo-breaking 1964 beating of England.

■ Robin Chisholm kicks clear in a 1958 Test v. France . . . with a good view of Murrayfield's old wing stand in the background.

■ The Queen visited Murrayfield as part of her Coronation Tour in 1953, again giving us a good view of the stand.

■ As London Scottish scrum-half Ken Spence shows during practice, rugby would go ahead at Murrayfield whatever the weather.

■ The game took place on February 28th, 1953. A 26-8 win for Ireland and Spence's only Five Nations cap.

■ This picture gives a good view of the instantly recognisable clock tower which stood atop the Railway End at Murrayfield for more than 60 years.

It was built thanks to a donation in 1929 by Sir David McGowan, former chairman of the SRU, and is still at the stadium, although it was moved to the rear of the East Stand during the 1990s remodelling.

The on-field action shows Ken Scotland kicking down the line v. Ireland on February 25th, 1961, a 16-8 win for the home side.

SCOTTISH RUGBY
IN THE BLACK AND WHITE ERA

The terrible toll of the wars

THE War Memorial Arch at Murrayfield tells of a terrible toll of rugby men. It marks the sacrifice of the 31 Scottish internationals killed in the Great War, 1914-18, and a further 15 who died in the Second World War.

Scotland's losses in the wars were generally high. Men flocked to the cause in proportionally high numbers north of the Border.

In the highly-pressured recruiting drives for the first war, men were encouraged to join up in groups of friends, fellow villagers, or sporting team-mates. They were gathered in "Pals Battalions" where they fought together and died together.

The entire Watsonians first XV volunteered in 1914, and of the more than 200 registered players London Scottish had (spread across four senior teams) in 1913, only four men ever took the field for the club after the war. A quite incredible 69 of them had been killed.

And more Scottish rugby international players died than any of the other Home Nations. England lost 27 internationals in the first conflict, then 14 in the second.

Of the Scots who were killed in the first war, 26 of the 31 were officers.

The 12-foot stone arch doesn't carry the names of the fallen because more rugby men than those who were internationals gave their lives. The arch stands for all who made the ultimate sacrifice.

The memorial was originally erected at Inverleith in 1921, and transferred to Murrayfield in 1936.

It now faces Roseburn Street, at the corner of the South and East stands.

Next time you visit, pay your respects to the fallen.

IN PROUD MEMORY OF
THE SCOTTISH RUGBY MEN
WHO GAVE THEIR LIVES
IN THE GREAT WAR
1914-1918

HONOUR ALSO THOSE   1939-1945   WHO FOLLOWED THEM

DARK BLUE BLOOD
SCOTTISH RUGBY
IN THE BLACK AND WHITE ERA

Chapter 3

Oh Flowers of Scotland

THE international game has grown massively in importance and as the game's foremost focus of interest.

It was always the pinnacle of the sport, but with the establishment of The World Cup, the Six Nations, and TV audiences, and most tellingly the money that has been poured on to the professional game, we are in a different universe compared to the way rugby was in the amateur era.

You'll have been to Murrayfield. You will know this is true.

Scotland matches on our home turf are now among the great events marked on the nation's sporting and social calendars.

But long before the accountants got a hold of it the national team was always a matter of immense pride among players and fans alike.

There is a passion surrounding an XV in dark blue shirts that is almost religious. There is a fervour in the crowd that is almost worship.

There is also something hugely dignified about a Scotland rugby team. Victory is strived for with every muscle, every sinew straining. But if the team gives their best yet comes up short, there will still be honour and the players will conduct themselves with gentlemanly sportsmanship.

After the final whistle.

■ **March 27th, 1971. It's a try! Scotland's combative winger Billy Steele runs in a score . . . in a game that appears to feature just two players.**

■ The world's first ever international. Scotland v. England, on March 27th, 1871. A challenge from five captains of Scots rugby teams had been made on the pages of sporting periodical *Bell's Weekly*. The teams agreed to play two 50-minute halves, 20 men per side, and by "rugby rules", at Raeburn Place home of Edinburgh Academicals.

The Scotland team, wearing brown shirts and cricket flannels, was (not in left-to-right order here): William Brown (Glasgow Acad), Thomas Chalmers (Glasgow Acad), Alfred Clunies-Ross (St Andrews University), Thomas Marshall (Edinburgh Acad), William Cross (Merchistonians), John Arthur (Glasgow Acad), Francis Moncreiff, captain (Edinburgh Acad), Angus Buchanan (Royal HSFP), Andrew Colville (Merchistonians), Daniel Drew (Glasgow Acad), William Forsyth (Edinburgh Uni), James Finlay (Edinburgh Acad), Robert Irvine (Edinburgh Acad), William Lyall (Edinburgh Acad), James Mein (Edinburgh Acad), John MacFarlane (Edinburgh Uni), Robert Munro (St Andrews Uni), George Ritchie (Merchistonians), Alexander Robertson (West of Scotland), John Thomson (Glasgow Acad/St Andrews Uni).

■ February 15th, 1958. Scotland battle their way to a 12-8 victory over the touring South Africans at Murrayfield. Tackling during the game was described as "keen".

■ **Scotland lined up that day:** R. W. T. Chisholm (Melrose) A R. Smith (captain, Gosforth), G.D. Stevenson (Hawick), J.T. Docherty (Glasgow HSFP), T.G. Weatherstone (Stewart's College FP), G.H. Waddell (Devonport Services), J.A.T. Rodd (United Services, Portsmouth), H.F. McLeod (Hawick), N.S. Bruce (Blackheath), T. Elliot (Gala), M.W. Swan (Oxford University), J.W.Y. Kemp (Glasgow HSFP), A. Robson (Hawick), J.T. Greenwood, Perthshire Academicals), G.K. Smith (Kelso).

■ More of that keen tackling during Scotland v. South Africa, 1958.

■ Though there be rain, sleet, snow, gale-force winds, mud, blood, hell or high water — get to the ball first.

Rugby is played in all weathers, it suits all sorts and shapes of players from sturdy props and hardy backs, to balletic wingers and highly-skilled ball distributors . . . all of them working together.

It is the perfect sport. It requires athleticism, team-work, speed and thought.

This race for the ball is from the Scotland v. Ireland Five Nations match of February 23rd, 1957.

The narrowest of wins, 5-3, to the Irish lads. Great game though.

■ Two shots from Scotland v. France, in the Five Nations, January 9th, 1960.
A hard-fought 13-11 win for the visitors.

■ Scotland's First XV, 1961.

Back, from left: Ronnie Thomson (London Scottish), Eddie McKeating (Heriots), John Douglas (Stewarts), Mike Campbell-Lamerton (Blackheath), Frans Ten Bos (Oxford University, Iain Laughland (London Scottish).

Sitting: George Stevenson (Hawick), Ken Smith (Kelso), Hugh McLeod (Hawick), Arthur Smith (Edinburgh Wanderers), Norman Bruce (London Scottish), Dave Rollo (Howe of Fife), Ken Ross (Boroughmuir).

On ground: Alex Hastie (Melrose), Ken Scotland (London Scottish).

■ The ref intervenes in a little "afters" in the
Scotland v. Ireland match of February 15th, 1961.

■ Two shots of Scotland v. South Africa, January 23, 1961. The tourists won 12-5, completing a clean sweep of victories over the home nations.

■ **Forced into touch. The powerful Springboks v. Scotland at Murrayfield in 1961 . . . in the days when newspaper photographers were free to run along the touchlines in search of a good angle.**

■ **Scotland v. Wales, Murrayfield, February 13th, 1961. Wales win the ball from a scrum, but the kick for touch is charged down.**

■ Scotland v. Wales, February 3rd, 1963. A painful 6-0 win for the Welshmen in the Five Nations. Walter Thomson, writing as The Sunday Post's Fly-Half, described the Scots' performance as "slovenly".

■ Scotland's Ronnie Thomson tackling Bill Morris.

■ **Scotland, January 18th, 1964. Scotland 0, New Zealand 0.**

A snarling, battling, stubborn Scottish display in which the pack, every man an amateur, gave away an average of 12 lb and yet dominated.

As The Sunday Post's Fly-Half commentator wrote after the game: "Wha Daur Meddle Wi' Me?"

Scotland, back, from left: RC Williams (referee), Jim Shackleton (London Scottish), Jim Telfer (Melrose), Billy Hunter (Hawick), Peter Brown (West of Scotland), Jim Fisher (Royal High School FP), Tremayne Rodd (London Scottish), A.S. Davidson (touch judge).

Middle: Ian Laughland (London Scottish), Christie Elliot (Langholm), Norman Bruce (London Scottish), Brian Neill (captain, Edinburgh Academical), Gregor Sharp (Stewart's College FP), David Rollo (Howe of Fife), Tom Grant (Hawick).

Front: Stewart Wilson (Oxford University), Ronnie Thomson (London Scottish).

■ **April 17th, 1965. A line-out (left) and the final whistle celebrations as Scotland beat the touring Springboks 8-5 at Murrayfield.**

■ Left: Scotland v. France, 1965. Right: Scotland v. Ireland, 1967. Old fashioned line-outs, before lifts came into the game, were very different, and more competitive, things to what they are today.

■ A Scot, Charles Rutherford, was a prime mover in establishing rugby in France and captained the French in a match against Canada in 1902. But have the French been grateful over the years? No. They are always tough to play against. But this game, on January 15th, 1966, was a tight 3-3 draw at Murrayfield.

■ Scotland v. France, January 13th, 1968. Both teams wore black armbands in memory of French players Guy Boniface and Jean-Michel Capendeguy who had died in separate car crashes within the first two weeks of 1968.

■ Two photos of Scotland v. France at Murrayfield, January 10th, 1970. Scotland narrowly lost 11-9, although missed several chances to kick their way to a win. The teams, as printed in newspapers of the time, are a good example of a tradition almost always used when reporting rugby. Players were listed by their initials, however many they had, and surname. No first names were given. Most other sports, except cricket, would routinely have players listed using only surnames.

No one working in newspapers can now remember who started presenting rugby players in the same manner as cricketers. It was probably intended as a mark of respect, or deference, for the gentlemen amateurs who played the game. The ties between cricket clubs and rugby XVs, of course, are many.

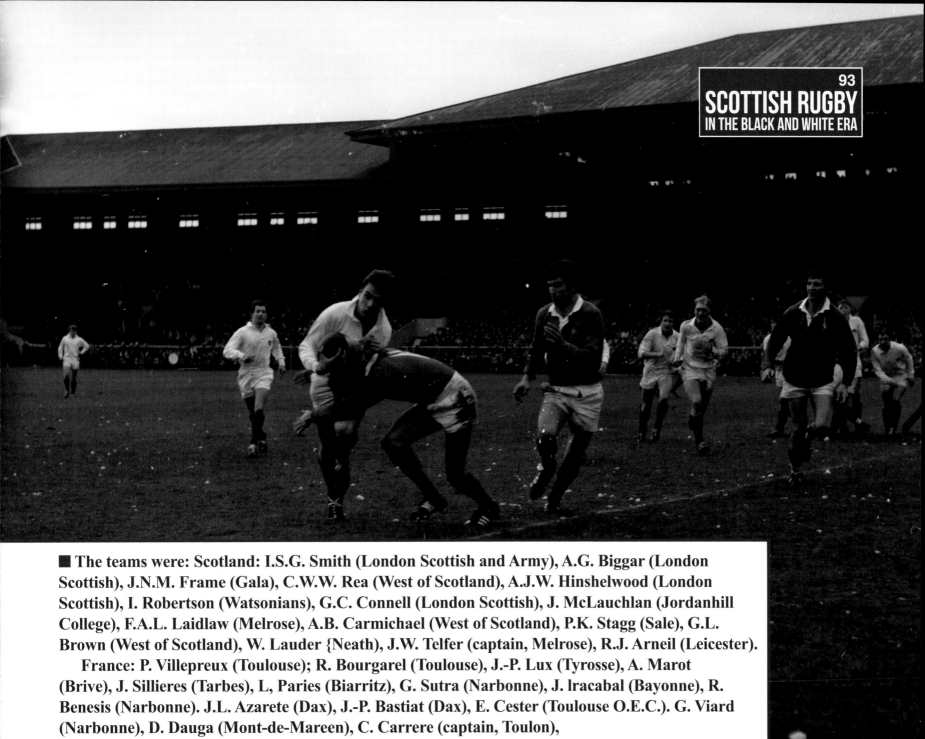

■ The teams were: Scotland: I.S.G. Smith (London Scottish and Army), A.G. Biggar (London Scottish), J.N.M. Frame (Gala), C.W.W. Rea (West of Scotland), A.J.W. Hinshelwood (London Scottish), I. Robertson (Watsonians), G.C. Connell (London Scottish), J. McLauchlan (Jordanhill College), F.A.L. Laidlaw (Melrose), A.B. Carmichael (West of Scotland), P.K. Stagg (Sale), G.L. Brown (West of Scotland), W. Lauder {Neath), J.W. Telfer (captain, Melrose), R.J. Arneil (Leicester).

France: P. Villepreux (Toulouse); R. Bourgarel (Toulouse), J.-P. Lux (Tyrosse), A. Marot (Brive), J. Sillieres (Tarbes), L, Paries (Biarritz), G. Sutra (Narbonne), J. lracabal (Bayonne), R. Benesis (Narbonne). J.L. Azarete (Dax), J.-P. Bastiat (Dax), E. Cester (Toulouse O.E.C.). G. Viard (Narbonne), D. Dauga (Mont-de-Mareen), C. Carrere (captain, Toulon),

Referee: Air Commodore G. C. Lamb (England).

■ **March 1st, 1975. Dougie Morgan kicks for goal during Scotland's 12-10 victory over eventual Five Nations champions Wales. The 104,000 Murrayfield crowd would remain a world record attendance for a rugby match for 25 years.**

■ As well as Dougie the other Scotland players are Gordon Brown, David Leslie, Nairn McEwan, Billy Steele, Ian McLauchlan, and Jim Renwick.

■ Another Scotland v. Wales, 1975 photo. Fly-half Phil Bennett flies through the air with the greatest of ease. That Welsh team took some stopping!

■ The Welsh side of the 1970s were a joy to watch, one of the greatest sides to ever grace the game. But Scotland's record against that "second golden era" side (the first golden era was roughly 1900-1919) wasn't bad at all. These photos are Murrayfield 1973 (above), a 10-9 win for Scotland, and (right) the previously mentioned 1975 win.

■ Two photos of Australia's northern hemisphere tour of 1975-76, which was referred
actually played a game, going home when the Second World War broke out. Scotland
the left, playing the Australians is always a physical encounter, they try to take a

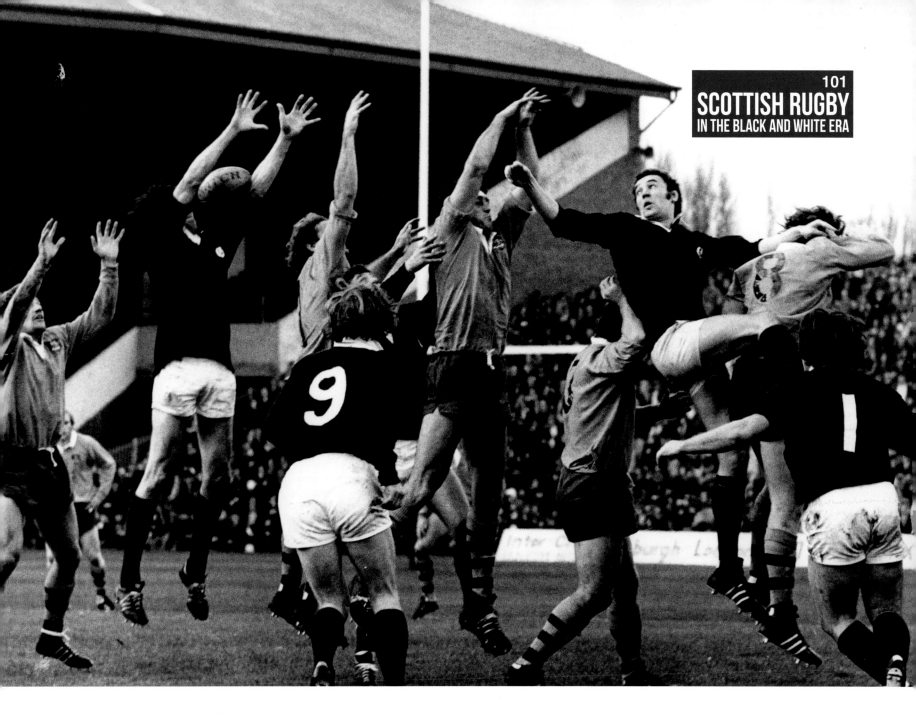

to as "The Sixth Wallabies", although some might say fifth as the Second Wallabies never
saw them off 10-3 at Murrayfield on December 6, 1975. As can be seen from the photo on
stranglehold on games. Mind you, they couldn't find any other way to stop Colin Telfer.

■ Two shots from the 1984 Grand Slam-winning win over France at Murrayfield. Jim Calder went over for a try, and Peter Dods' accuracy with the boot (five penalties and the conversion) won Scotland their first clean sweep since "The Immortals" nearly 60 years previously, and the first Triple Crown since 1938.

It was a grand day.

■ Scotland's Five Nations pool, 1984 was: Jim Aitken (captain, Gala), Roger Baird (Kelso), Jim Calder (Stewart's Melville FP), Alister Campbell (Hawick), Bill Cuthbertson (Harlequins), Colin Deans (Hawick), Peter Dods (Gala), Gordon Hunter (Selkirk), David Johnston (Watsonians), Euan Kennedy (Watsonians), Roy Laidlaw (Jedforest), David Leslie (Gala), Iain Milne (Heriot's), Steve Munro (Ayr), Iain Paxton (Selkirk), Jim Pollock (Gosforth), Keith Robertson (Melrose), John Rutherford (Selkirk), Alan Tomes (Hawick).

■ If you're going to win a Grand Slam, then you have to beat Wales. It sounds obvious, but rest assured this task will never be an easy one.

Scotland's famous 1984 slam was founded on an opening day 15-9 victory in Cardiff. It wasn't a great Welsh team, by their standards, but not a bad one either. They would go to Twickenham and score a 24-15 win the following month.

This photo shows: Back, from left: Irish touch judge, Irish fourth official, Steve Munro, Iain Milne, Euan Kennedy, Iain Paxton, Alan Tomes, Bill Cuthbertson, Jim Calder, David Leslie, Irish referee Owen Doyle, other Irish touch judge.

Front: Gordon Hunter, Norrie Rowan, Douglas Wylie, John Rutherford, Colin Deans, Roy Laidlaw, Jim Aitken, Peter Dods, David Johnson, Roger Baird, Keith Robertson, John Beattie, Rob Cunningham.

DARK BLUE BLOOD
SCOTTISH RUGBY
IN THE BLACK AND WHITE ERA

Chapter 4

The Auld Enemy

THERE is a special rivalry that exists between Scottish and English rugby men. It's (almost) always sporting, of course, but there is an added edge to encounters between the Auld Enemies that has, throughout the history of the game, made this a must-win fixture.

The Scots say the English are arrogant, the Sassenachs say the Scots have a chip on their collective shoulder. Perhaps they're both right.

Some would say it is a David v. Goliath thing, but that's just the English inferiority complex.

Perhaps it is political, perhaps it is a cultural difference, perhaps it is that ill-defined socio-economic thing. No matter what label you wish to apply it is mainly about respect, or sometimes a lack of it.

If any man, especially a rugby man, feels he has been treated shabbily then he will want to repay that slight. It is beneath a sportsman to offer disrespect in return, but it becomes his duty to run over his opponent as if he wasn't there.

It's about pride. It's about playing for that shirt with the thistle on the chest. It is about taking the best your opponent has to offer and beating him anyway.

It's about having dark blue blood.

■ **Scotland v. England, March 23rd, 1954.**

■ England won this Calcutta Cup joust 8-6 at Murrayfield in 1968, but (opposite page) Scotland showed them that this uppityness wasn't to be tolerated with a 14-5 trouncing two years later.

■ A trial of strength during the Calcutta Cup match of 1962.

■ A try! Scotland on their way
to the 1964 win over England.

■ David Whyte plunges over the line to score the winning try in the 1965 Calcutta Cup, clinching three victories in a row over "them".

■ These pages (and the next four) are photos of the 1972 rout of England. The 23-9 score sealing our fourth successive win, the longest ever run of Scottish Calcutta Cup victories.

■ A damaged but atmospheric and movement-filled photo of the Calcutta Cup encounter of February 2nd, 1974. A famous 16-14 win for Scotland.

■ Two of the great names of Scottish rugby in action against the Auld Enemy in the 1980s. Left: Roy Laidlaw gets scheming in 1988. This page: John Jeffrey charges down a kick in 1986.

DARK BLUE BLOOD
SCOTTISH RUGBY
IN THE BLACK AND WHITE ERA

Chapter 5

Faces in the Crowd

PLAYING the game is a fine thing. An end in itself. But playing in front of a crowd elevates the experience for players and spectators alike.

A game of rugby is a spectacle. It requires a degree of commitment from players that will always be fascinating to watch.

So there is a special air, an atmosphere to a rugby crowd that exists but rarely in sport. There is an appreciation of just what it takes to play the game. There is an understanding and a reflection of the controlled aggression, the self-discipline required.

There is support, and fervent support at that, but also an appreciation that this is a sporting contest. It is a healthy atmosphere, an event all the family can attend.

The game is honest and fair. The immense physical effort the game requires is appreciated. Good play is applauded, "gameness" is acknowledged. The match may be fierce and the crowd partisan. But there will always be that special rugby culture.

Rugby is a game in which the crowd joins the players in displaying the true spirit of what sport should be.

The faces you'll see on these pages are enjoying themselves. The photos are of past times, of course, but they were great days, great victories, great celebrations, and (most of all) great memories.

Remember when the game was like this?

■ **Melrose Centenary Sevens, 1983.**

A cold weather crowd
wrapped up warm at
Mansfield Park.

■ Slightly warmer weather, or at least warm enough for
picnic baskets, at what appears to be the Melrose Sports,
before the Greenyards stand extension in the late 1950s.

■ Tension in the crowd while the 1962 Calcutta Cup encounter teeters its way to a 3-3 draw.

	GOALS	TRIES	POINTS
SCOTLAND	1		3
ENGLAND	1		3

■ **Murrayfield flags fly two years later as Scotland rout the Auld Enemy 15-6.**

■ **What a day it was. An elated crowd converge on the pitch to celebrate that 15-6 trouncing of England in 1964, the first victory over them for 14 long years.**

■ **1970. Scotland 14, England 5.**
A good day was had by all.
Except the English.

■ March 17, 1984. A group of fans among the massed tartan gathering for the 1984 Grand Slam-winning game against France at Murrayfield.

■ December 1978. A healthy crowd of Aberdonians gathers at Linksfield Stadium to watch The All Blacks beat the North & Midlands Select 31-3.

The Granite City isn't usually renowned as a rugby town, but some schools gave children the afternoon off for the occasion of the New Zealand tourists coming to play.

To the surprise of some, the game thrives in the north, though it is a long way from Scotland's rugby heartlands.

■ Occasionally, as in this 1988 photo, odd English people would turn up on the shallow slopes of Murrayfield to learn from people who really know about the game.

And sometimes they brought anti-vegetarianism banners with them. No one knows why.

■ It isn't often that faces in the crowd can actually be named, but there are several well-known Borders folk in this photo of the 1995 Jed Sevens. The on-pitch action shows Gavin Dalgleish of Gala getting away from Kelso's Clive Millar. Just above Gavin are John Jeffrey's mother and father Margaret and Jimmy. The man behind Margaret (to the left) in the bonnet is Michael Johnstone from Kelso, and the lady wearing sun glasses is Francis Cook from Hawick. Next to Margaret Jeffrey is former Kelso president Archie Stewart. Above Clive Miller is George Haig, nephew of Ned Haig, the man who invented Sevens rugby.

ower

DARK BLUE BLOOD
SCOTTISH RUGBY
IN THE BLACK AND WHITE ERA

Chapter 6

When Giants Strode the Land

SCOTTISH RUGBY'S far off history (before the 1950s, for our purposes) tells of giants. The players of old were men of indescribable strength, who performed Herculean feats, and played only great games. The rain was wetter, the glaur was thicker, and every member of every opposition team was made of iron.

There are stirring tales told of the old gods, Angus Buchanan, Francis Moncrieff, Ian Smith, Phil Macpherson, Jock Beattie, Jimmie Graham, and their like.

And that is how it should be. The stories of those bravest of heroes deserve only to grow as years pass.

For we owe the game to those men. They played for honour, sportsmanship, and the thrill of the contest, not fame or fortune.

Things were different.

Players were strictly amateur, of course, and the organisation of the game was more amateur still. For years The Border League was the only opportunity for competitive domestic encounters.

Games outwith the South were "friendlies" (though often anything but friendly). Internationals were rare and the team-choosing process, done by selectors (though rarely the same set of selectors two games running), was haphazard.

But the game thrived. It found popularity in the Borders, especially, where it was a working-class game instead of the fee-paying schools sport that it was further north.

The popularity that was hard won in those days is the foundation upon which the modern worldwide game is built upon.

■ **Gordonians RFC 1st XV, September 21, 1949: Back, from left: F. Ogston, J. Reid (captain), A.P. McDonald, A. Craig, G.B. Farquharson, J.S. Taylor, D.J. McPherson, W.A. Walker.**
Front: N. Stott, W. Paisley, D.W. Ross, L. Frain, A.A. Tullett, A.J. Rennie, I. Elder.

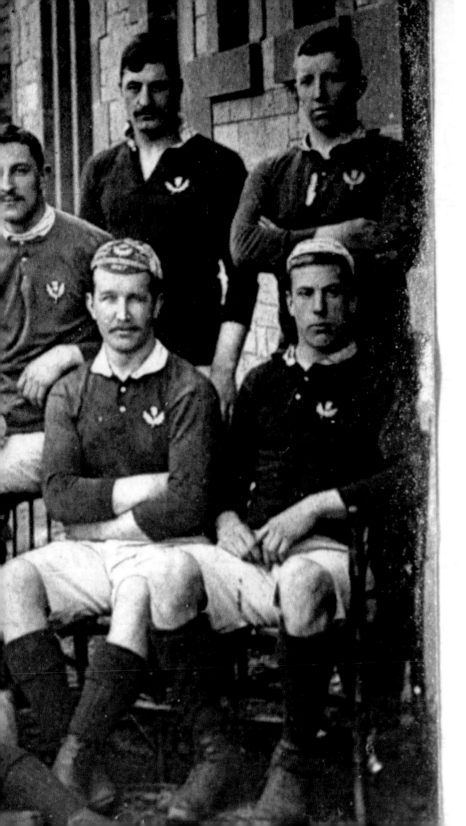

■ Scotland's team to play England on March 17th, 1894, kicking off at 10am before a crowd of 12,000.

This would be the last Calcutta Cup match to be played at Raeburn Place, though the first Scotland-England encounter under the new rules of three points for a try and two points for a conversion, rather than the other way around. The game ended as a 6-0 victory for the home side, securing Scotland's second Triple Crown.

The Scottish team that day (although not in left-to-right order in this photo) was: Robert "Judy" MacMillan (Edinburgh University), John Boswell (West of Scotland), Gregor MacGregor (Cambridge University), Herbert Leggatt (Watsonians), William Neilson (London Scottish), William Gibson (Royal High School FP), William Wotherspoon (West of Scotland FC), George Campbell*, William Cownie (Watsonians), James Gowans (Cambridge University), Henry Menzies, John Simpson, Henry Gedge (listed for London Scottish and Edinburgh Wanderers), Bill McEwan (Edinburgh Academicals), Gordon Neilson (Merchistonians).

*Club sides are not available for all players.

Scotland beat Wales 18-8, on February 9th, 1901, at Inverleith, on their way to a fifth championship win and a third Triple Crown.

The star of the tournament was Jimmy Gillespie of Edinburgh Academicals, who scored 22 points.

Also in the side was David Bedell-Sivright, the only Scotsman ever to win three Triple Crowns and reported to be the most ferocious, hardest man ever to play for Scotland.

He was a larger-than-life figure who, reportedly, after a few refreshments, once fell asleep on the Edinburgh tram tracks. Startled awake, he was said to have rugby-tackled the poor horse that was drawing an oncoming tram.

A surgeon in the Navy, he died of septicaemia, aged 34, during the Dardanelles Campaign in 1915.

Back, from left: David Bedell-Sivright (Cambridge Uni), Jimmy Ross (London Scottish), John Bell (Clydesdale), Andrew Flett (Edinburgh University), Robert Stronach (Glasgow Acads), Alexander Duncan (Edinburgh University), Alec Timms (Edinburgh University), Alfred Fell (Edinburgh University).

Front: John Dykes (Glasgow HFSP), Jimmy Gillespie (Edinburgh Acads), Mark Morrison, captain (Royal HSFP), Phipps Turnbull (Edinburgh Acads), Alex Frew (Edinburgh University).

On ground: William Welsh (Edinburgh Acads), Francis Fasson (Edinburgh University).

■ The 1906-07 South African touring side were the first to earn the name The Springboks, and garnered great respect for their rugby. They won 26 of their 29 games, drawing 3-3 with England and hammering some of Britain's district sides. The only Test they lost was this game to Scotland, in the unfamiliar surroundings of Hampden Park, on November 17th, 1906.

Scotland's 6-0 win was thanks to tries from Alexander Purves of London Scottish, and the remarkable Kenneth MacLeod. The swerving run MacLeod embarked upon to score is often described as breathtaking — as was his entire sporting career. He won 10 caps between 1905 and 08, but retired from the game aged 20, as his father feared he might be seriously injured, as his two elder brothers had been while playing rugby.

But he wasn't finished there. He scored 3,458 first-class runs as a cricketer, also taking 103 wickets for Cambridge University and Lancashire. He then played association football for Manchester City, and a few years later was the amateur golf champion of the province of Natal.

He died in 1967 but his feats saw him, rather deservedly, inducted into the Scottish Sports Hall of Fame in 2010.

■ The two teams that day. Back, from left: W.A. Burmeister, K.G. MacLeod, D. Brookes, L.M. Spiers, H. Corley (referee), D. Brink, J.C. McCallum, J.G. Scoular, H.A. de Villiers.

Middle: W.H.H. Thomson, A.F. Burdett, I.C. Geddes, J.A. Loubser, M.W. Walter, A.L. Purves, A.C. Stegmann, T. Sloan, A.F.W. Marsburg, G.M. Frew.

Front: D.S. Mare, D.R. Bedell-Sivright, H.J. Daneel, L.L. Grieg, H.W. Carolin, W.P. Scott, J.W.E. Raaff, H.G. Monteith, W.S. Morkel.

On ground: F. Dobbin, P. Munro, J.D. Krige.

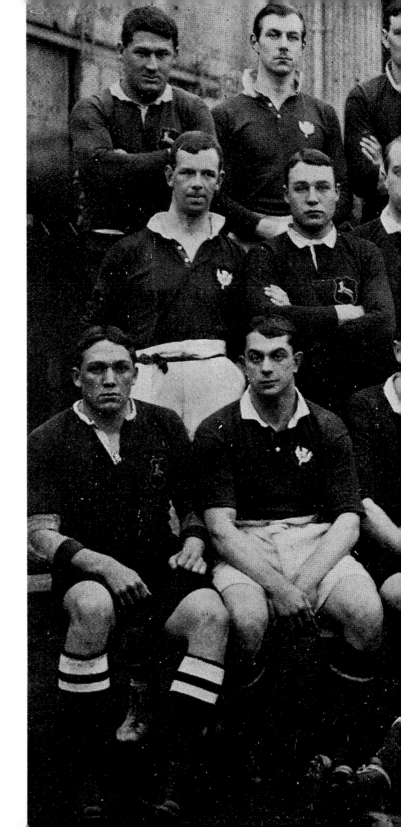

■ Scotland's first Grand Slam, and our only one for a further six decades, came in 1925, before the phrase "Grand Slam" had even been coined.

It was March 21st, the opening of Murrayfield, a red-letter occasion versus England, attended by 70,000 souls.

And what a game it was. Scotland were behind three times, before a 14-11 victory was secured by stand-off Herbert Waddell's drop-goal (then worth four points) in the final five minutes.

The Flying Scotsman, Ian Smith was a pivotal figure in the 1925 Five Nations Championship. His 24 international tries is still a Scottish record (although now a shared one with Tony Stanger).

That team's feats earned them the title, "The Immortals", because through their fame they will live for ever.

■ This is the team that beat Ireland in Dublin on March 7th, setting up the chance of the slam. Back, from left: James Dykes, Jimmy Nelson, David MacMyn, James Scott, James Ireland, Robert Howie, Ian Smith.

Front: George Aitken, Johnnie Wallace, John Bannerman, Dan Drysdale, John Buchanan, Doug Davies.

On ground: Herbert Waddell, John Paterson.

■ No rugby internationals were played during the war. People, quite understandably, had other things on their minds. But rugby can't be kept down. The British Army had a match against France at the Parc des Princes on January 1st, 1945. The French, despite a difficult preparation period involving Nazi occupation of their country, won 21-9.

The Brits used an imaginative re-naming ploy to become the British Empire Forces, sneaking some Kiwis and Springboks into the team, to play France again on April 28th, 1945, and win 27-6.

The following year, the "Victory Internationals" still weren't regarded as official, so no caps were given. Not all of the players had been demobbed, especially from the Pacific theatres of war. For this reason, the games were billed slightly differently. This photo, taken on March 30th, 1946, was termed a Scotland XV versus a Wales XV.

There were enough New Zealand armed forces stationed in the UK to make up a "Kiwis" team and a Scotland XV beat them 11-6 at Murrayfield on January 19, 1946. But it would be a stretch to claim this as a win over the full All Blacks side.

The important thing was that, despite the rucks and mauls of a world war, rugby was back.

■ Scotland's 1946 XV. From left: Gus Black, Alexander Watt, Richard Aitken, Doug Smith,

Charlie Drummond, David Deas, J. Kirk, John Orr, Russell Bruce, Dod Lyall, Doug Elliot, Keith Geddes (captain), William Munro, Ian Lumsden, Ian Henderson.

■ **North District Trial Blues, October 20th, 1948. Back, from left: W.A. Walker (Gordonians), J.D. Chalmers (Aberdeen Grammar School FP), D. Stuart (Aberdeen University), G. Smylie (Gordonians), W.A. Ross (Gordonians), J.S. Taggart (Aberdeen Uni.), J. Milne (Aberdeen GSFP), J.S.G. Munro (Aberdeen GSFP). Front: J. Young (Aberdeen Wanderers), A.P. McDonald (Gordonians), K.G. Stephen (Gordonians), A.G. Craig (Aberdeen GSFP), D.N. Georgeson (Aberdeen GSFP), K.W. Hunter (Aberdeen GSFP), F. Clark (Aberdeen Uni.).**

153

■ **North District Trial Whites (to play the Blues on the left). Back, from left: G.J. Joss (Aberdeen Uni.), A.H. Tawse (Aberdeen GSFP), J. Davidson (Aberdeen Wanderers), R.M. Bruce (Gordonians), A. Tullet (Gordonians), W.L. Connon (Aberdeen GSFP), I. Elder (Gordonians). Front: R.F.F. Steven (Aberdeen Uni.), E.A. Campbell (Aberdeen Wanderers), E. Buthlay (Aberdeen GSFP), E. Hunter (Aberdeen GSFP), R.F. Buthlay (Aberdeen GSFP), J.C. Hunter (Aberdeen GSFP), W.D. Allardice (Aberdeen GSFP). Again, you can see the usage the photos have had over the years.**

■ South of Scotland representative team for a match v North at Rubislaw Playing Fields, Aberdeen, on November 12th, 1949.

Back, from left: J. Johnston, W.R. Scott, H. Balsom, J. Heggarty, R.L. Wilson, G. Burrell, J.B. Lees. Front: J. Wright, O. Turnbull, G. Tait, S. Coltman (captain), C.W. Drummond, D.M. Hogg, G.G. Lyall.

DARK BLUE BLOOD
SCOTTISH RUGBY
IN THE BLACK AND WHITE ERA

Chapter 7

The 1950s, a tough time for hard men

THE worst of times . . . and yet some of the best of times, to mangle Mr Dickens' famous line.

International rugby, as played by Scotland, was old-fashioned and ineffective. The Dark Blues suffered 17 defeats in a row between February 1951 and February 1955, and didn't beat England from 1951 to 1964.

But the latter half of the decade saw improvement. If there was no win in the Calcutta Cup, there were three draws and some very fine players were emerging.

Ken Scotland, Robin Chisholm, Arthur Smith, Ian Thomson, Jim Greenwood and the Hawick Hardman Hugh McLeod (among many others) arrived on the scene.

McLeod is pictured several times in this book and deserves a special mention. These were the days of amateur rugby and McLeod was a plasterer to trade, having to fit in his rugby around his job.

At five foot nine, and nearly 16 stone, he was described as "rather harder than teak".

He won 40 caps, making him the world's most-capped forward at the time, and is a giant figure in the history of his hometown club, Hawick.

In today's world, he would be a renowned superstar. In those days, he ran a sports shop on Oliver Place after giving up plastering, and was seen on his bike every day on Hawick High Street.

You know you've made a bit of an impression when your home town names a street (Hugh McLeod Place, up in Stirches) after you.

■ It was never easy to stop Hugh McLeod when he got going.

■ Two South of Scotland XVs, a year apart — 1956 (above) and 1957 (right). There are some fine players here, but none more celebrated than Hugh. He is on the far left at the back, above, and third from right in the back row of the 1957 photo.

■ **Midlands XV selection on October 10th, 1953 — another of the helps-make-up-our-minds games beloved by selectors, played at Linksfield Stadium, Aberdeen. The Whites, back, from left: Unknown, C.W. Bravin (Dunfermline Rugby Club), J.K. Donaldson (Perthshire Academicals), J.K. Mearns (Panmure Rugby Club), A. McNicoll (Harris Academy FP), J.R. Andrew, J. Greenwood (Dunfermline), Dr F.H. Moore (Perthshire Acads). Front: Unknown, Unknown, Unknown, A.K. Fulton (captain, Dollar Academicals), Unknown, A.S. Hay (Perthshire Acads), J.P. Allardyce (Harris Academy FP).**

■ The Blues for the same game. Back, from left: A.R. Pate (Highland Rugby Club), E.H. Cruickshank (Aberdeen Grammar School FP), P.G.H. Younie (Aberdeen Wanderers RFC), A.I. Cheyne (Aberdeen University Rugby Club), E. Mitchie (Aberdeen University), C.D. Mowat (Aberdeen GSFP), M. Wolfe Murray (Aberdeen Wanderers RFC), A.B. Mulholland (Gordonian RFC). Front: K. McLean (Aberdeen University), A. Tullett (Gordonian), D.N. Georgeson (Aberdeen GSFP), W.D. Allardice (Aberdeen GSFP), D.H. McPherson (Gordonian), I.L. Robb (Aberdeenshire RFC), G.R. Ferries (Aberdeen Wanderers).

162

■Among the autumn leaves . . . Midlands Rugby Select, October 23, 1954. Back, from left: J. Johnston, J. Greenwood, I.S. Gloag, J.G.H. Fenton, R.H. Gibson, R.C. Whittet, J.R. Andrew, J.W. Hay, J.K. Morrison. Front: C.W. Bravin, G.W. Adam, E. Rogers, R. Sutherland, W. Steven, D.M. Brien.

■ A rather poor quality shot of Hugh McLeod (second from right) with Hawick teammates, from left,
George Stevenson, Adam Robertson, Jack Hegarty and Oliver Grant, at Inverleith in 1959.

■ **Perthshire Academicals, November 1957.** Back, from left: R.D. Williamson, G.L. Crozier, A.G. Stirrat, A.C. Glen, J.N. Smith, D.A. Smith, G.R. John, M. McLaughlan, Sandy Fraser (touch judge). Front: N.R. Marr, D.M. Brien, C. Hay, A.S. Hay, K.J. Donaldson, E.E. Campbell, D.G. Mowatt.

■ **Howe of Fife, February 1958. Back, from left: J. Clark, A.S. Mathieson, J. Steven, W. Steven, A. Adamson, G.B. Wilson, W. Dodds, I.A. Ross. Front: D.S. Gough, A.L. Watt, W.Y. Bell, T.R. Pearson, I. Donaldson, A.C. Mackie, C.C. Brunton.**

■ **This is a South Select with not much info, it is from the 1950s.**

■ **South District, November 7th, 1959. Back, from left: Brian King (Hawick), Derek Brown (Melrose), JimTelfer* (Melrose), Charlie Murdie (Jedforest), George Stevenson* (Hawick), Keith Anderson (Gala), John Cunningham (Hawick), Ronnie Grieve (Hawick). Front: Oliver Grant* (Hawick), Wattie Hart*(Melrose), Dougie Lightbody (Jedforest), Adam Robson* (Hawick), Ian Hastie* (Kelso), Jim Gray (Hawick), Eck Cassie (Melrose).** *Denotes internationalist.

DARK BLUE BLOOD
SCOTTISH RUGBY
IN THE BLACK AND WHITE ERA

Chapter 8

The 1960s. The doldrums

THE 1960S was a bit of a doldrums time, not just for Scottish rugby but British rugby as a whole.

Started by the Welsh, but spreading out quickly, kicking became very important. The ball spent a lot of time in touch and games turned into line-outs displays. It took a rules change to remedy this, although that didn't arrive until 1968.

Hawick dominated The Borders League, with a good team, and there was healthy domestic competition.

Reorganisation of the Scottish game was needed, though the official Scotland-wide championship wasn't to begin until the early years of the following decade.

But some very good players were around. Jim Telfer was making his mark as one of our nation's all-time-great leaders of men. Ken Scotland was redefining the full-back role, and

Sandy Carmichael won the first of his 50 caps in 1967.

■ **Dundee High School FP, September 8th, 1965. Back, from left: G.G. Burnett, D.J. Tasker, J.D. Orr, G.L. Potter, G.G. Robertson, G.D. Duncan. Middle: M. Hardie, G.F. Ritchie, R.J. Leslie, V.A. Barrow, W.F.S. Neillie. Front: J.H.R. Wright, H.L. Findlay, C.W.W. Rea, J.C. Scott.**

■ **South of Scotland Select, November 1960.**

The South, where rugby is a way of life, were always able to put out an incredibly strong representative XV.

Back, from left: Eck Cassie (Melrose), Ronnie Cowan* (Selkirk), Ronnie Grieve (Hawick), Drew Mathieson (Kelso), Nat Carson (Gala), Charlie Stewart* (Kelso), Derek Brown (Melrose), Oliver Grant* (Hawick).

Front: Davie Chisholm* (Melrose), Ken Smith* (Kelso), Christie Elliot* (Langhom), Robin Chisholm* (Melrose), George Stevenson* (Hawick), Eck Hastie* (Melrose), Hugh McLeod* (Hawick).

*Denotes international.

■ The North fell 22-9 to the South African tourists on January 25, 1961.

■ **Hawick Rugby Football Club, March 1962.**

■ **Kirkcaldy Rugby Football Club, November 1962.**

■ A damaged photo (apologies especially to Ken Ross) of the Scotland XV ready for a trial match during the terrible winter of 1963. These photos have had long working lives in archives.

This was a game about to be played on an iron-hard surface, covered with an inch of snow, during the coldest winter of the 20th Century. But it was "game on" — no complaints, no holding back.

Back, from left: Jim Shackleton, Tom Grant, Mike Campbell-Lamerton, Ron Thomson, Frans Ten Bos, Iain Spence, Norman Bruce, William Watherston.

Front: Iain Laughland, David Chisholm, Tremayne Rodd, Ken Scotland, Ken Ross, David Rollo, Charles Hodgson.

■ **Howe of Fife Rugby Club, October 16, 1964, including international prop forward David Rollo. Back, from left: W. Bell, J. Kinnes, R. McGregor, E. Cameron, G.C. Stewart, R.H. Gibson, W. Steven, K. Todd, D. Rollo. Front: A. Imrie, A. Mitchell, T. Pearson, W.W. Law, G. Stephens, J. Clark.**

178

■ **The Broughty Ferry Boys. Panmure RFC, November 20, 1966. Back, from left: I.B. Rae, B.N. Bowman, K.J. Mowbray, J.R. Scott, A.H. Pattullo, D.K. Rae, W.S. Pale, G.R. Wilson, A.J. Lyburn. Front: A.J. Black, D. McLennan, I.B. Fisken (capt), J.K. Morrison, G.M. Lyle, I.G. Stevenson.**

■ North of Scotland XV which met the Springboks at Linksfield Stadium on Wednesday, January 25th, 1960. Back, from left: I.R. MacDonald (Aberdeen Grammar FP), W.M. Johnston (Dunfermline RFC), W.S. Glen (Perthshire Academicals), D.M.D. Rollo (Howe of Fife), A .Fraser (Perthshire Academicals), R. Steven (Howe of Fife), G.P. Hill (Gordonians), M.G.H. Gibb (Aberdeen Grammar FP). Front: D.J. Whyte (St Andrews Uni), A.G.D. Whyte (Gordonians), J. Coletta (Gordonians), JC Craig (Harris Academy FP), I.G. McCrae (Gordonians), A. Bryce (Dunfermline), R.J.C. Glasgow (Gordonians).

■ Midlands Rugby Select for the 1964 District Championships. Back, from left; D.M. Brien, A.J. Nicol, D.M.D. Rollo, G.H. Tyrie, J. Beveridge, J.B. Stevens, R.J.C. Glasgow, R.T. Leslie. Front: C.C. McLeod, A.W. Sinclair, E.C. Reoch, C.P. Carter, J.A. Rhind, C.W.W. Rea, J.H.R. Wright.

■ **The Fife XV that beat Angus and Perth XV 25-9 in the Midlands trial at Monymusk, Dundee, on October 11th, 1967. Back, from left: G.W. Robertson, J.M. Moffat (both Kirkcaldy), J.B. Blackwood (Howe of Fife), C.G. McLeod (Madras FP), P.J.G. Smith (St Andrews University), W.G. Hall (Howe of Fife), K.M. Watson (Madras FP), M. Waddington (Howe of Fife), R. Jack (Madras FP). Front: G.T. Owens (Kirkcaldy), A.S. Fraser (Madras FP), J. Braid, D.M.D. Rollo (captain) (both Howe of Fife), L.F. Hunter, R.A.M. Scott (both Madras FP).**

■ St Andrews University team of February 1964. Back, from left: G.F. Ritchie, P. Beetlestone, R. Steven, G. Lorimer, A.J. Gainer, B. Andrew, C.P. Carter, N. Allan, J.C. Smith. Front: D.T.M. Salmond, B.W. Brown, J.D. Cumming (captain), T.J. Ellesemere, M.G.S. Debenham, M.I.C. Singer.

■ **This page and next — Australia's 1966-67 European tour took them to Linksfield Stadium, Aberdeen, to play**

the North of Scotland Select. The Wallabies won, as might have been expected, but only by a narrow 6-3 margin.

■ **Hawick RFC, 1965-66. Winners of the Border League, the Scottish Unofficial Championship and the Sports at Kelso, Gala, Melrose, Hawick, Jedforest, Langholm and Huddersfield.**

Back, from left: J. Auchinleck, V. Sharp, G. Lyall, D. Deans, D. Cranston, A. Bannerman, R. Grieve, J. Gray.

Middle: A. Graham, P. Robertson, N. Suddon, J. Scott, W. Hunter, R. Brydon, T. Dawson, R. Welsh.

Front: J. Hay, G. Stevenson, E. Broatch (captain), H. Laidlaw (president), W. Jackson, H. Whitaker. C. Telfer.

.

■ **North & Midland team pictured at Linksfield Sports Stadium, Aberdeen, February 1964. Back, from left:
G.P. Hill, R.J.C. Glasgow, D.J. Rankin, J.P. Pashley, I.C. Wood, I.C. Spence, J.B. Steven, K.H. Wood. Front: I.C.
Wood, I. Robertson, B.W. Brown, K.J.F. Scotland, C.P. Carter, J.A. Rhind, I.C. McRae.**

190

■ Howe of Fife XV, December 3rd, 1966. Back, from left: W. Hall, J. Lindsay, W. Waddington, J. Barr, J. Kirkhope, J. Braid, A. Logan, L. Scorcjemaki. Front: W. Young, K. Crighton, J. Manson, A. Jack, M. P. Melville, A. Wales, M. Bollins.

■ **Kirkcaldy Rugby Football Club First XV, season 1966/67. Back, from left: H. Moultrie (president), P. Tate, D. Sellar, C. Scobie, J. Thomson, R. Briggs, R. Drummond, W. Yule, I. Donaldson, J. Anderson, G. Curry (secretary). Front: W. Couper, I. Baptie, G. Owens, R. Bease (captain), M. Lockhart (vice-captain), J. Grieve, L. Hutchison.**

■ Morgan Academy FP, March 1969. Back, from left: A. Clapp, C. Burns, T.W. McLean, D.E. Booker, D.J. Davidson, J.C.S. Robertson, I.J. Kerr, K.H. Bagat, W.G. Lindsay, I.G. Grieve. Front: J.B. Imlay, B.S. Hendrie, A.F. Gouick, I.B. Petrie, A.N. Geddes.

■ **Hawick v. Daniel Stewarts FP, early 1960s. Hawick players from left to right: Derek Grant, Oliver Grant, Billy Hunter, Hugh McLeod and Dougie Jackson with the ball..**

DARK BLUE BLOOD
SCOTTISH RUGBY
IN THE BLACK AND WHITE ERA

Chapter 9

The 1970s. The mean machine

STRANGE ideas such as "change" begin to be talked about in the 1970s.

The game was organised into a formal six-league structure for the 1973-74 season. This suited the "open" clubs (those not tied to drawing their numbers from the former pupils of schools).

This may have been a break from tradition, but the game itself emerged the stronger. For the first time since World War 1, the national team was made up predominantly of players from Scottish clubs.

Scotland became the last of the Home Nations, in 1971, to appoint a national coach, Bill Dickinson, although his official title was "adviser to the team captain".

Bill proved to be remarkably good at the job, a tactical genius and a leader of men. His enthusiasm, and game-winning success, changed Scottish national rugby for ever.

The mean machine pack, led by "Mighty Mouse"Ian McLaughlan was one of the most feared units in the world game. And the Scottish rugby public loved it. No team came to Murrayfield and had an easy time.

Men such as Andy Irvine, Broon fae Troon, Alastair McHarg, and Sandy Carmichael were doing great things.

■ **Right: Scotland v. Ireland, February 1973.**

196

■ **October 10, 1972. The North Region "Blues v. Whites" selection game. The Whites, back, from left: W. Stephen (Gordonians), C. Paterson (Aberdeen Grammar School FP), H.M. Brown (Glenrothes), J. Adams (Glenrothes), W.B.F. Morgan (Dunfermline RFC), G. Spry (Aberdeen GSFP); I. Gray (Aberdeen GFP); M.R.F. Clark (Panmure). Front: A.S. Fraser (Highland Rugby Club), R.W. Duncan (Aberdeen GSFP), A. Bissell (Perthshire RFC), A. Leighton (Glenrothes), G. Slater (Gordonians), P.E. Snape (Gordonians), S.A. Ballantyne (Madras).**

■ **North Region Blues from the same game. Back, from left: D. Aitchison (Highland Rugby Club), T. Dunlop (Dundee University), S. McKenzie (Ross Sutherland Rugby Club), G. Skinner (Gordonians), J. McGregor (Gordonians), D.W. Arneil (Dunfermline), I.G. McCrae (Gordonians), T.E.R. Young (Moray Rugby Club). Front: A. Hardie (Aberdeen GSFP), J. Baird (Dunfermline), C. Snape (Gordonians), J. Officer (Montrose Rugby Club), F.M. Ellen (Highland Rugby Club), D. Leslie (Dundee HSFP), C. Watt (Gordonians).**

198

■ **Dundee University Rugby Team, February 6th, 1973. Back, from left: Douglas Mayne, Jim Yarwood, Dick Welbury, Rob Wilford, Mike Nash, David Nicholson, Willie Henderson, Mike Telford. Front: Ian Kettle, David MacRobert, David Alexander, Jon Westbury, David Black, Alan McHoul, David Perry.**

■ A line-out during the game between Perthshire and Howe of Fife at the North Inch, Perth, on Saturday. January 4th, 1975.

■ Schools, and FP clubs are the lifeblood of rugby, especially outside the Borders area. The game would have long ago withered and died in some areas but for the dedicated on- and off-field endeavours of such organisations.

This is Harris FP on May 2nd, 1974. Back, from left: W. A. Booker, A. T. K. Rodger, J. Farnan, R. Johnstone, J. McPherson, G. Moffat, D. W. S. Wright, A. Booker, J. C. C. Jeffrey. Middle row: M. S. Doig, E. G. Greig, D. W. Black, R. L. Lamb (captain), A. Alexander, J. M. M. McIntosh, A. G. Robbie. Front, on ground: R. McClure, M. Sievwright, R. Millar, R. S. Haggart.

■ The North Midlands
Select ready to face the
tourings All Blacks side
at the old Linksfield
Stadium, Aberdeen, on
December 5th, 1978.

Back, from left:
A.J. Croll, D.W.
Arneil, S.F. Mackenzie,
R.C.F. High, C.E.
Snape (captain), I.G.
McCrae, J. Adams,
A.D.G. Mackenzie,
I. Sutherland, J.A.
Hardie, R.D. Young,
J. Imrie, S.R. Irvine,
W.A. Brand, G. Brown,
A. Dunlop, I. Paxton,
C.F. Watt, G.W.
Smylie, A. Ingle-Finch,
P. Robertson.

The New Zealnders
won 31-3, but then
that touring side, the
8th All Blacks, would
be the first to do the
"slam", winning all
four Tests against the
home nations.

■ **Madras College FP v. Heriots, at St Andrews, September 30th, 1978.**

■ **The North Midlands team that topped the 1974-75 Inter-District Championship (shared with Glasgow).**
Back, from left: R.D. Young (Dunfermline), D.G. Leslie (Harris FP), T.D. Dunlop (Dunfermline), C.E. Snape (Gordonians), J. Sheddan, C.A. Galbraith (both Dunfermline), J.R. Rawlinson (Perthshire RFC), G.M. Halliday (Highland Rugby Club), C.F. Watt (Gordonian), N.A. MacEwan (Highland). Front: J. Adams (Dunfermline), I.G. McCrae (Gordonians), T.E.R. Young (Moray RFC), W.D. Aitchison (Highland), D.W. Arneil (Dunfermline).

■ **Gordonians RFC, at Seafield, September 10th, 1976. Back, from left: S. Irvine, A. Croll, G. Calder, J. Officer, M. Corrie, P. Snape, G. Slater, A. Hardie, S. Wilson, C. Rae, S. Cusiter, C. Snape, M. Stewart, I. McCrae, D. Donald.**

DARK BLUE BLOOD
SCOTTISH RUGBY
IN THE BLACK AND WHITE ERA

Chapter 10

The 1980s. Domestic high-water mark

THE 1984 Grand Slam was long awaited, and the result of the clinching game took a long time to flow Scotland's way, too.

We hadn't won a slam for nearly 60 years and, facing France at Murrayfield on March 17th, 1984, the chance looked to be slipping away.

But the lads scored 18 points in the last 14 minutes of the game to send the crowd wild.

The 33-6 humbling of England at Twickenham in 1986 must also stand out as a hight point.

John Rutherford, Matt Duncan and the Hastings brothers put together a second-half annihilation that will still be talked of in 100 years' time.

The domestic game was thriving, with the '80s sometimes described as the high-water mark for Scottish club rugby.

Border clubs dominated the Scottish championship, Gala, Hawick and Kelso sharing out the title over the decade. The Border Championship enjoyed success alongside the national competition.

But the central belt clubs were on the rise too, and would soon come to prominence.

■ **Jed-Forest v Currie in 1988, at the Riverside in Jedburgh. A match played in such glaury glory that even the referee is filthy.**

■ **Muddy marvellous. The photographer looks like he'll be on the end of this pass during Melrose v. Jed-Forest at the Greenyards, January 1988.**

And the groundsman will have been expected to perform a miracle with the chewed-up morass that is left to him after the game.

■ Hawick entertain Heriots in 1981.
From left: Andy Irvine (Heriots), Derek Turnbull (Hawick), Jim Renwick (Hawick) Kevin Rafferty (Heriots), Harry Burnett (Heriots), Paul Hogarth (Hawick), and Billy Murray (Hawick).

■ Jed v Gala — Roy Laidlaw about to kick.

■ The Aberdeen Select v. Exiles Boxing Day
match has been a tradition since 1930. It is played in
all weathers. In this 1981 photo, Exiles captain Stewart Irvine
makes a break across the Rubislaw playing fields snowscape.

■ It took a few years after the introduction of the National Leagues for Gordonians to really make their mark, but 1980 changed all that. The club had gone open in 1974, winning Division III, then the team pictured above made it to the top flight in season 1979-80. Back, from left: F.W. Paterson, D. Lawson, J. Pringle, J.B. Morrison, G. Hill, I.E. Alllan, J.G. Dow. Front: J. Rennie, W. Russell, I.C. McCrae, R.J.C. Glasgow, A. Leiper, J. Coletta, M. Taylor, A.B. Mulholland.

■ The 18-year-old Doddie Weir, with David Little, in a 1988 Melrose v. Kelso game.

■ **International Greens.** In November 1984 there was a gathering of Hawick men who had also represented Scotland.

Back, from left: Billy Hunter (first cap 1964), George Stevenson (1956), Jim Renwick (1972), Rob Welsh (1967), Alistair Cranston (1976), Robin Charters (1955), Norman Suddon (1965), Derek Deans (1968), Jack Hegarty (1951), Ian Barnes (1972).

Middle: Sean McGaughey (1984), Doug Davies (1922), Willie Welsh (1927), Hugh McLeod (1954), Stuart Coltman (1948), Adam Robson (1954).

Front: Derrick Grant (1965), Colin Deans (1978), Allan Tomes (1976), Alistair Campbell (1984), Colin Telfer (1968).

■ The North Midlands side beaten 34-9 by Edinburgh at Rubislaw, Aberdeen, on October 30th, 1982.

Back, from left: Charles Hay (Panmure RFC), David Graham (Highland Rugby Club), Alan Croll (Gordonian RFC), David Whiteford (Highland), Donald Flockhart (Highland), Brian Bell (Howe of Fife RFC), Jack Dobie (Madras College FP), David Paton (Gordonian), Graham Philip (Gordonian), Kevin Wyness (Aberdeen Grammar School FP).

Front: Jack Imrie (Howe of Fife), Alister Wemyss (Highland), Michael Stewart (Gordonian), Jerry O'Rourke (Highland), John Bryce (Alloa Rugby Club), John Murray (Aberdeen GSFP), Callum Mackintosh (Highland).

■ The Hawick squad who clinched the club's 10th Scottish Division 1 championship in season 1985-86. The Greens were always the benchmark for club success in Scotland.

Back, from left: Paul Nolan, Jim Hay*, Nick Bannerman, Stuart Hogg, Sean McGhaughey*, Jock Rae, Andrew Johnston, Richard Bannerman, Doug Waldie.

Middle: Derek Willison, Ronnie Nichol, Derek Turnbull*, Alistair Campbell*, Allan Tomes*, Jock Mallin, Tony Stanger*, Colin Deans*, Brian Renwick.

Front: Kenny McGhaughey, Robbie Douglas, Keith Mitchell, Keith Murray*, Colin Easton (captain), Derek Deans* (president), Paul Hogarth, Greig Oliver*, Colin Gass, Donald Whillans.

*Denotes international.

■ 1986. Jed's Roy Laidlaw, hotly pursued by Hawick's John Hogg, Keith Murray and Alistair Campbell.

■ **Another hard-fought Jed v. Hawick encounter, in September 1988.**

■ **Edinburgh beat South at Netherdale to win the 1986-87 District Trophy.**

■ **December 1986. North & Midlands v. South.**

■ Rugby is played all over Scotland. This is Orkney Rugby Football Club in 1987, celebrating the 20th anniversary of their first ever game.

Rugby has a proud history on the islands. Kirkwall Football Club played a match (v. Thurso) in 1879, and also took on other teams, though KFC didn't survive.

The present club was founded in 1966, after Mr Peter McKinlay placed an advert looking for players in the local newspaper.

The first game was a 20-5 win over Caithness at Pickaquoy, on April 1st, 1967 — and the club has gone from strength to strength from there.

■ This is a 1988 reunion marking the 25th anniversary of Melrose's 1962-63 championship win.

The squad are, back, from left: Norman Rutherford, Jimmy Doyle, Gordon Tweedie, Ian Rutherford, Dod Haldane, TD Wight, Frank Laidlaw*.

Third Row: George Lackie, Jim Telfer*, Mike Laidlaw, Joe Swinton, Bert Blacklock, Ian Johnstone, Alec Hastie*, Les Allan*, Davie Hogg.

Second row: Robin Chisholm*, Eric Allan, Mack Brown, Derek Brown, Sandy Galbraith, Ell Allan, John Crawford, Ronnie Dagg, Jimmy Johnstone*, Kenny Monks, Rob Innes, Norman Elliot, David Broomfield.

Front row: Adam Crawford, Sandy Gibson, Arthur Brown, Davie Chisholm*, Jack Dunn, Charlie Mitchell, Jim Hogg.

*Denotes internationalist.

DARK BLUE BLOOD
SCOTTISH RUGBY
IN THE BLACK AND WHITE ERA

Chapter 11

The 1990s. Time to go pro

THE decade opened with a bang. Scotland enjoyed one of its landmark rugby years.

Flower of Scotland was officially adopted as the anthem of the national side and was belted out by the Murrayfield crowd on March 17th, 1990, the Grand Slam decider against the Auld Enemy at Murrayfield. Some would say the 13-7 win was Scotland's greatest ever game.

The '90s was a time of great change for Scottish Rugby Union, of course. Professionalism arrived.

After the incredible success of the '95 World Cup the game changed for ever.

It became a global, big-money business. For better or worse (and there are still arguments) Scotland had to fall into line.

The International Rugby Board's decision to go pro wasn't popular with the SRU, but was inevitable. "Shamateurism" was ended, the threat of players being tempted to Rugby League was halted, though it had rarely been a threat north of the Border.

■ **Craig Chalmers kicking for Melrose, v. Jed, for the 1990 League championship.**

FOR FITNESS & HE
SCOTCH

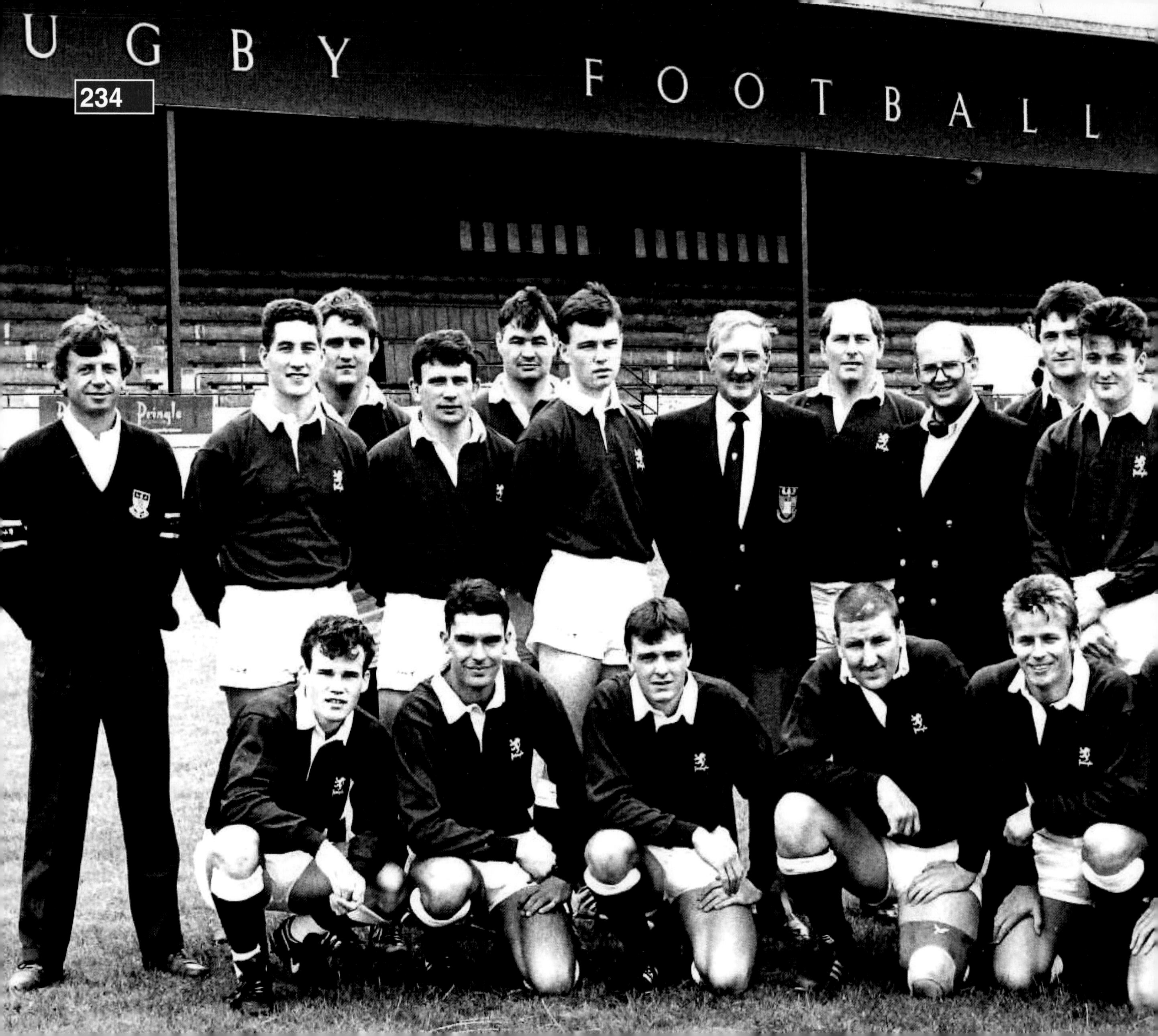
UGBY FOOTBALL
Pringle

Hawick Rugby Football Club

HAWICK are the big boys. They are powerhouse that lies within the heartland of Scottish rugby. They have the history, they have the tradition. The donning of a dark green jersey is regarded as an honour.

Other teams measure themselves against the club they call "The Green Machine".

The town of Hawick is Scotland's rugby capital.

And if the Robbie Dyes at Mansfield Park declare you "a good fitbaa player", then you can regard yourself as a good player.

■ **The Greens get a set of new strips in 1990.**

236

■ Melrose 1990.
Winners of the Border
League and Southern
Division 1.

■ **Gavin Hastings was one of the biggest figures in Scottish rugby in the 1990s, scoring a quite incredible 667 points over the course of his international career.**

■ **Another Scotland great of the 1990s, Andy Nicol, in action.**

■ St Boswells men Brian Anderson with ball, and Arthur Moore beside him, v. Peebles, January 1990.

■ Muddy Melrose men Andrew Kerr, Doddie Weir, Carl Hogg and Euan Simpson. in a match v. Selkirk in January 1993.

■ Everyone has to start somewhere. There are hundreds of men and women, parents, teachers and volunteers who aren't mentioned in this book, and probably won't ever be mentioned in any book, who are doing incredibly good work to train, inspire and help the game at grassroots level.

Every great player started out as a kid on a damp patch of grass, wondering what on earth he or she was supposed to do with this strange, oval-shaped ball.

The game of rugby, of course, started in a school, and many of our famous old Scottish clubs are Former Pupils organisations. There probably wouldn't be much to Scottish rugby without all of those clubs.

It is, after all, a game for the players.

■ Gala Academy's 1991 Scottish Schools' Cup winning team. Back, from left: Stuart Aitchison, Chris Dalgleish, Jonny More, Michael Blues, Stevie Rodkiss, Gregor Townsend (on shoulders), Cammy Bell, Kevin Rutherford, Bruce Chalmers, Richard Bramble. Front: Roy Hislop, Gary McQuary, Gareth Brown, David Paterson, Scott Easson.

Gregor Townsend became head coach of the Scottish national side in May 2017

CHALMERS Mc QU...
SELF · DRIVE · CONTRA... HIRE · VAN

■ A Carl Hogg try helps Melrose retain the Border League championship, v. Gala, in 1991.

■ The men from the Greenyards won it again in 1993. Quite an achievement for a town of just 2,000 souls.

■ **Orkney RFC, October 17th, 1990. The 1991-92 was the club's Silver Jubilee season and they finished in a very respectable third place in their first season in the North League, having previously competed in the Highland League.**

■ September 1994. Gavin Hastings, in his Watsonians days, playing against Melrose.

■ The South team that beat Edinburgh at Murrayfield to win the 1990/91 Inter-District championship.

Back, from left: Gary Isaacs (Gala), Jim Hay* (Hawick), Derek Turnbull* (Hawick), Charlie Stewart* (president of the SRU, formerly of Kelso), John Jeffrey* (Kelso), Jock Millican* (SRU board member, formerly of Edinburgh University), Gordon Marshall* (Selkirk), Scott Nichol* (Selkirk), Gary Waite (Kelso), Craig Redpath* (Melrose).

Front: John Laing (Gala), Doddie Weir* (Melrose), Peter Dodds* (Gala), Gary Armstrong* (Jedforest), Craig Chalmers* (Melrose), Iwan Tukalo* (Selkirk), Mark Moncrieff (Gala).

*Denotes internationalist.

■ Gary Armstrong kicks at the Jed Sevens, 1994. It was a bit damp at the time.

■ A little bit of Melrose
magic against Currie,
in March 1994.

■ Hawick's 1996-97 league championship-winning side.

Back, from left: Alistair Imray, John Graham, Grant Blacklock, Derek Turnbull, Ian Elliot, Mick Robertson, Brian McDonell, Kevin Reid, Andrew Johnstone, David Grant.

Front: Grant Harris, Jim Hay, Keith Suddon, Colin Turnbull, Brian Renwick, Scott Welsh, John McDevit, Greg Oliver, Fraser Jack.

SRU TENNE
SEASON 199

■ The wee town of Melrose is really a village.

But Melrose Rugby Football Club consistently punches way above its weight.

The Greenyards lads regularly win silverware and just as regularly step up to become internationalists.

It must be something they put in the Tweed water.

■ Melrose RFC won the Scottish Cup in 1997 to complete a "double".

DARK BLUE BLOOD
SCOTTISH RUGBY
IN THE BLACK AND WHITE ERA

Chapter 12

The All Blacks' visits to Scotland

THEY come with that aura, they come to win, and every game against them is an event.

We've been fascinated by The All Blacks for more than a century, since "The Originals", the first New Zealand side to tour the UK in 1905-06 (see next page).

Their tours are much anticipated events and they will attract huge crowds wherever they go.

They visit Scotland on a regular basis and the Tests against them are lifetime highlights for players — but the regional games are just as eagerly anticipated and always very well attended.

That peculiar intensity they bring to every game finds a match in the Scottish psyche.

The likes of a North Midland Select standing firm before the Haka, against a backdrop of Aberdeen multi-storey flats, is quite a sight.

But then, New Zealand owes its rugby to Scotland. The man who introduced the game to the islands, Charles Monro, was the son of an Edinburgh Scot, Sir David Monro, descendant of a long line of renowned Scottish doctors.

■ **Right, a re-touched photo (with crop marks) of the February 27th, 1954, Scotland v. All Blacks Test, which was part of the 1953-54 Britain, Ireland, France and North America tour. The All Blacks won by the narrowest of margins, 3-0, that day. But all the praise was for the resilience and strong play of the Scots.**

■ The respect that goes with The All Blacks is founded on legends of the "Original All Blacks" tour of the British Isles, France and North America, 1905-06. The New Zealanders played 35 games, including Tests against all the Home Nations, and lost only once, a hotly-disputed 3-0 reverse at the hands of Wales. In total, the tourists scored 976 points and conceded 59.

The tour turned the rugby world on its head. The first match was against Devon, runners-up in the English County Championship. The 55-4 rout of the Devonians was such a surprise that some newspapers printed the score the wrong way around, believing initial reports must be incorrect. But NZ went on to trounce England's county sides by record scores, creating a sensation that swept the UK. Crowds for the tour games rocketed.

The first Test was against Scotland on November 18th, 1905. This (right) was the Scotland team. The home team acquitted themselves well, leading 7-6 with ten minutes to play, but the All Blacks eventually won 12-7. The tourists played England two weeks later, before a crowd estimated at 100,000, and won 15-0.

The Originals tour was the first time the All Blacks name was used and the first time the UK saw the Haka. New Zealand's reputation as the benchmark for world rugby has remained ever since.

■ Back, from left: William Russell, Tennant Sloan, Lewis MacLeod, Ken MacLeod, Louis Greig, John MacCallum, John Scoular. Front: James MacKenzie, Ernest Simson, William Scott, David Bedell-Sivright, Leonard West, William Kyle, John Simson. On ground: Pat Munro.

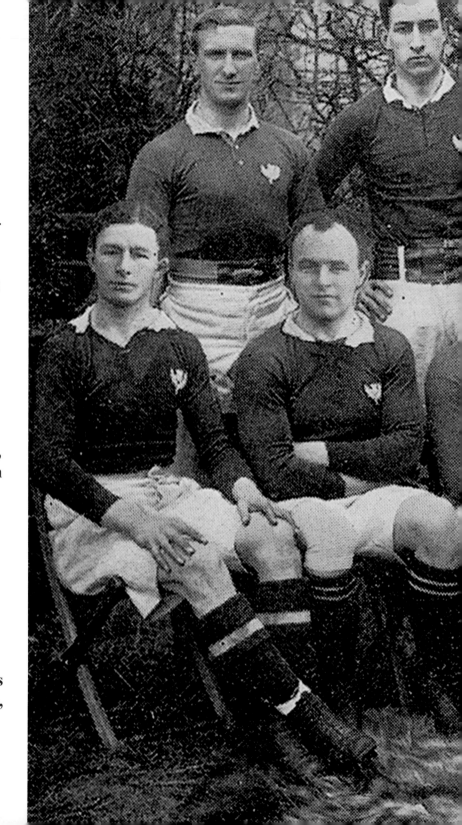

■ The Haka before the Test at Murrayfield on January 18th, 1964. The 0-0 draw that day was a landmark moment in rugby history. It remains the last time a match between two tier 1 international sides remained scoreless.

■ Another two shots from January 18th, 1964, with Scotland in their change kit. This was the only Test of that tour that the New Zealanders didn't win, and one of only two draws (the other was 1983) between the countries.

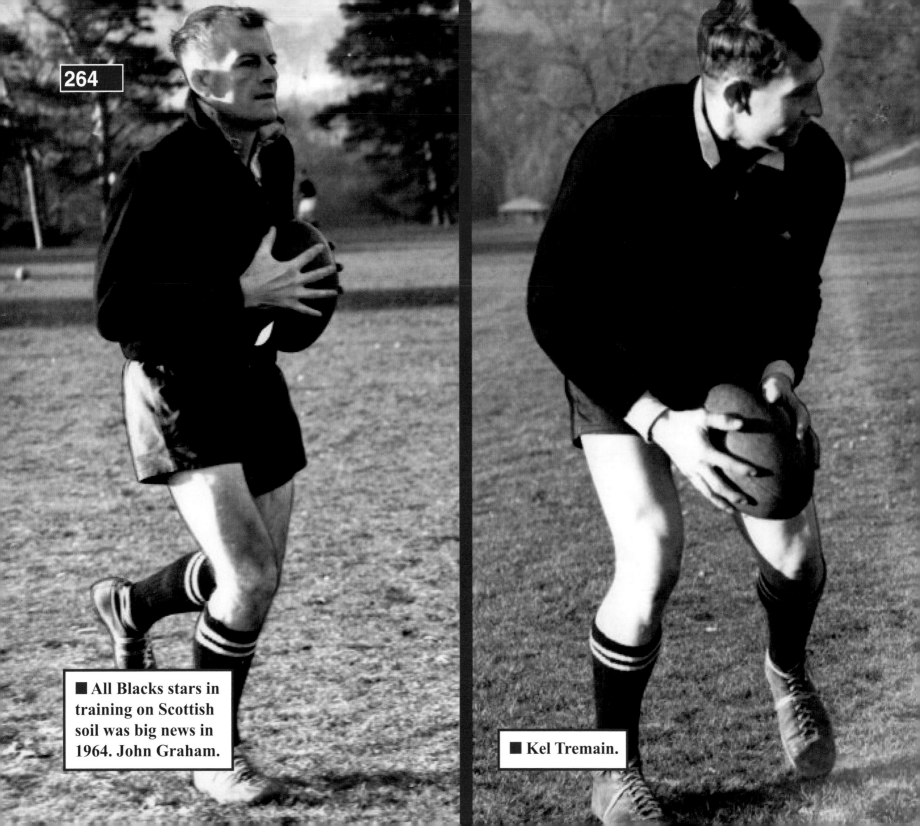

264

■ All Blacks stars in training on Scottish soil was big news in 1964. John Graham.

■ Kel Tremain.

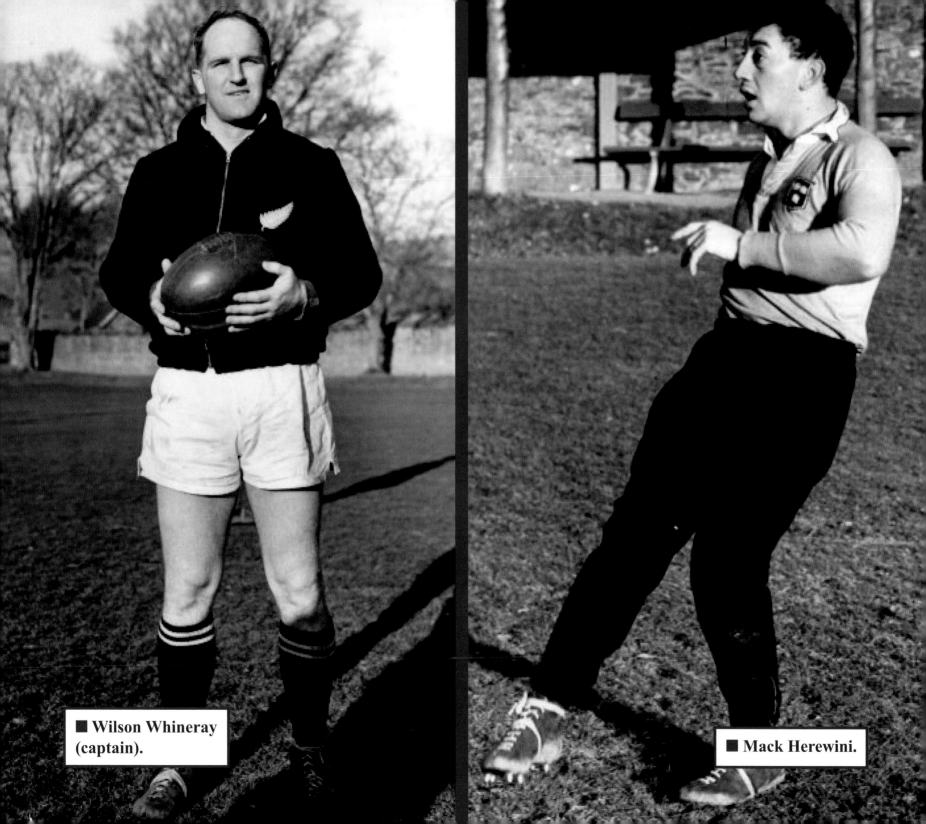

■ Wilson Whineray (captain).

■ Mack Herewini.

■ The Haka, a long way from home, before a 1978 tour match v. The North, in Aberdeen.

■ Scotland v. New Zealand is always an occasion.

The All Blacks will give everything they have in every Test. This, in turn, makes any side playing against them raise their game. The New Zealanders know this and accept it, and are made yet more determined to triumph. It's a self-feeding, cast-iron guarantee of entertainment for spectators.

These two pages, and the next four, hold images of Scotland v. The All Blacks, December 9th, 1978, an 18-9 win for the visitors on a day of torrential rain in front of a 70,000 Murrayfield crowd.

Scotland's team that day was: Andy Irvine, Keith Robertson, Jim Renwick, Alistair Cranston, Bruce Hay, Ian McGeechan (captain), Alan Lawson, Ian McLauchlan, Colin Deans, Bob Cunningham, Alan Tomes, Alastair McHarg, Mike Biggar, David Leslie, Gordon Dickson.

■ It will end in handshakes.

They are different teams, different hemispheres, different ways of approaching the game. But, Scotland or All Blacks, the spirit of rugby is always the winner.

Picture shows the final whistle of the Test v. the All Blacks 1964.

The Scots players (in white) from left are: Gregor Sharp (Stewarts FP), Tremayne Rodd (London Scottish), Jim Telfer (Melrose), Billy Hunter (Hawick), Brian Neill (Edinburgh Accies), Peter Brown (West of Scotland), Dave Rollo (Howe of Fife).

DARK BLUE BLOOD
SCOTTISH RUGBY
IN THE BLACK AND WHITE ERA

Chapter 13

The Sports, a grand day out

SEVENS rugby is good fun. It was an inspired invention, and (like many great inventions) is all thanks to a Scotsman.

In the very early years of the game, former Melrose RFC player Ned Haig suggested a sports tounament to raise money for his club.

Ned, a butcher to trade, hit upon the idea of seven men playing a 15-minute game instead of the established 15 men playing an 80-minute game.

Ned's idea was first tried out on April 28, 1883. It was an immediate success.

Gala, Hawick and Jed set up their own tournaments within a few years and after a few decades the idea spread around the world — though the original Melrose tournament and the Borders circuit remain the most prestigious.

There is a tradition of inviting teams from outwith the Borders area to take part in the best Sevens circuit in the world.

Many great sides with line-ups of legendary players, have come from New Zealand, France, Canada, South Africa, Hong Kong and all manner of other places to play.

Sometimes, even English teams are allowed in.

Anyone who has ever been to a Sevens festival will tell you it is a fantastic day out.

There are rumours of spectators taking alcoholic refreshment while attending, though this has never been proved.

■ **Harry Hogg at the Melrose Sevens, 1987.**

■ A team from Lothian & Borders Horse Regiment won the wartime Melrose Sevens in 1915. Note the recriting poster in the background. Back row, from left: W.D.L Cullen, Bill Kepp (although this player is also listed as Jock Smith), unidentified sergeant, Archie McNab, C. Clarke (listed as a Gala player). Front: J.A. (Jammy) Mann, W.R. Sutherland, A.P. Turnbull.

■ Right: Panmure RFC's Sevens side of 1969.

■ **Gala Sevens winners Hawick from the late 1950s (exact year unknown, Hawick won the Gala tournament in 1956, '58 and '59). Back: Ian Fraser, George Stevenson, Drew Broatch, John Cunningham. Front: Jack Hegarty, A. Robson, Jock Wallace. Right — Hawick's winning side of 1960.**

280

■ Big crowds always come out for The Sports.

284

■ **Dundee High School FP Sevens team, April 1964. Back, from left: C. Reid, V. Barrow, R. Leslie, D. Wright. Front: R. Byer, H. Wright (captain), K Wood.**

■ **Dundee High School FP Sevens team, September 1970. Back, from left: G.P.W. Hall, G.B.R. Cram, R.T. Leslie, A. Wallace, W.A. Masson (Stirling County). Front: K. H. Wood, R. C. Brickley, D. G. Coutts.**

286

■ Dunfermline Rugby Seven, April 11th, 1971. Back, from left: P. H. B. Hepburn, R. Watt, W. B. F. Morgan, W. G. Chisholm. Front: S. Buchanan, S. G. Fowler, P. Gibbons.

■ Morgan Academy FP at the North Inch Sevens, Perth, April 12th, 1958. From left: N. Davidson, W.B. Kydd, L.H. Mitchell, J.M. Pope, M. Henry, B.W. Mitchell, F.F.D. Stott.

■ **The British Lions team at the 1989 Earlston RFC Sevens, which was part of the Borders Sevens Circuit. The circuit has since expanded into a league format, known as the Kings Of The Sevens. The champions being the team that performs best over the 10-game series.**

■ Teams from all over the world are invited to Scottish tournaments, but Scots also regularly travel to tournaments overseas. This Borders team took part in the prestigious Hong Kong Sevens in November 1990. This was the tournament in which John Jeffrey temporarily became a Welshman after The Borderers were knocked out of the competition. John played for The Valleys due to injuries.

■ **London Scottish invaded from the south to win the Kelso Sevens in 1991.**

■ **Kelso took home the Melrose Sevens trophy six times in the 1980s. This is the 1980 champions.**

■ Hawick won the Gala RFC Sevens, the second oldest Sevens tournament in the world, in 1992.

■ Michael Dods hoists the Jed Sevens trophy for his home-town club Gala in 1994.

■ A Mexican Wave makes its way round the 1992 Melrose Sevens.

■ Jed v. Stirling County at the 1994 Selkirk Sevens.

■ Rugby club nights out are the stuff of legend — not just in Scotland, but across the world. Every club, every rugby nation, every time.

This is a fact known to all men.

Do they get out of hand at times? Yes they do. Are there sore heads and regrets (and sometimes consequences to be faced) in the morning? Yes there are.

Will this ever change? No.

This night out — Aberdeenshire RFC in 1986 — must stand as an illustration for all rugby nights out.

It was the only photo we could find that could be printed.

If you liked this book, you might also like these two . . .

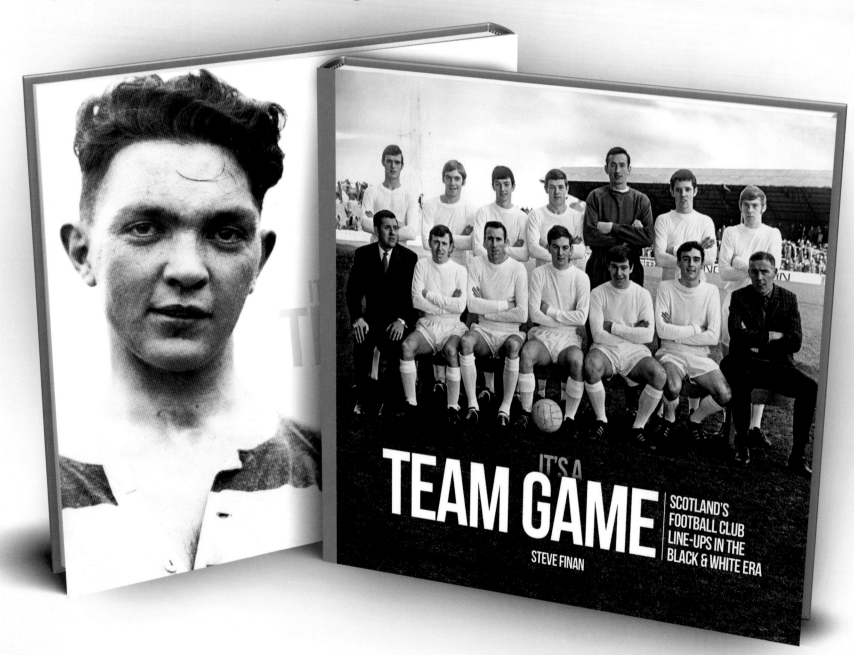

IT'S A
TEAM GAME

SCOTLAND'S
FOOTBALL CLUB
LINE-UPS IN THE
BLACK & WHITE ERA

STEVE FINAN

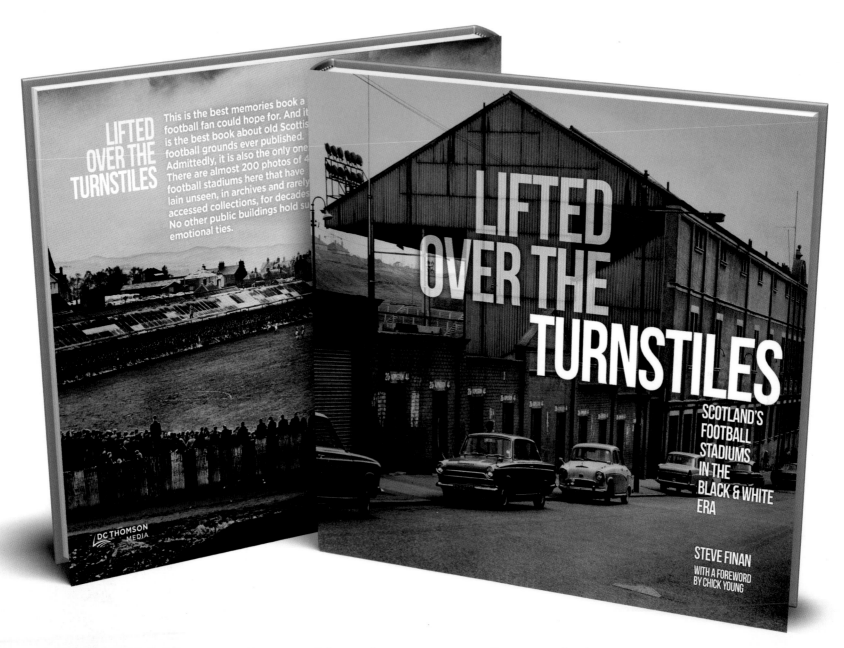

LIFTED OVER THE TURNSTILES

This is the best memories book a football fan could hope for. And it is the best book about old Scottish football grounds ever published. Admittedly, it is also the only one. There are almost 200 photos of 4 football stadiums here that have lain unseen, in archives and rarely accessed collections, for decades. No other public buildings hold su emotional ties.

LIFTED OVER THE TURNSTILES

SCOTLAND'S FOOTBALL STADIUMS IN THE BLACK & WHITE ERA

STEVE FINAN

WITH A FOREWORD BY CHICK YOUNG

Available from all good book sources, but quickest and most reliably from: www.dcthomsonshop.co.uk

Provenance

Should you wish to purchase a copy of a photo in this book, most are available to buy from:

DC Thomson

photoshopscotland.com

Pages 32/33, 40/41, 42/43, 45, 48/49, 51, 52/53, 54, 55, 63, 66/67, 68/69, 70/71, 72, 73, 74/75, 78, 79, 80, 81, 84/85, 86, 87, 88, 89, 90/91, 92/93, 94/95, 96/97, 98, 99, 100, 101, 102, 103, 107, 108, 109, 110, 111, 112/113, 114/115, 116/117, 118/119, 120/121, 122/123, 128, 129, 130/131, 133/134, 141, 152, 153, 154/155, 158, 160, 161, 162, 164, 165, 169, 172/173, 176/177, 178, 179, 180, 181, 182, 183, 184/185, 186/187, 189, 190, 191, 192, 195, 196, 197, 198, 199, 200/201, 220/221, 227, 238, 239, 257, 260/261, 262, 263, 264, 265, 266/267, 268/269, 270/271, 272/273, 279, 284/285, 286/287, 296,297.

Southern Reporter

tweedalepressnewsprints.co.uk

Pages 125, 138/139, 205, 210/211, 212/213, 214, 217, 218/219, 222/223, 224, 225, 226, 230/231, 232/233, 234/235, 236/237, 240,241, 242/243, 244, 245, 247, 248/249, 250, 251, 252/253, 254/255, 277,278, 280,281, 288, 290, 291, 292, 293, 294, 295.

Hawick Heritage Hub

hawickonline.com

Pages 10/11, 18/19, 20/21, 22/23, 34/35, 126, 127, 157, 163, 188, 193.

Scran Learning Culture Heritage

scran.ac.uk

Pages 12/13, 14/15, 16/17, 24/25, 26/27, 28/29, 36/37, 38/39, 44, 46/47, 50, 56, 57, 58/59, 82/83, 132, 136/137, 209, 274/275.

Rugby Relics

rugbyrelics.com

Pages 104/105, 142/143, 144/145, 146/147, 148/149, 150/151, 258/259.

Canmore Images

canmore.org.uk

Page 61.